MOBILE JOURNALISM

A Key Mass Communication Tool of the Future

MOBILE JOURNALISM

A Key Mass Communication Tool of the Future

DR RAHUL DASS

PRABHAT PAPERBACKS

Published by
PRABHAT PAPERBACKS
An imprint of Prabhat Prakashan Pvt. Ltd.
4/19 Asaf Ali Road,
New Delhi-110002 (INDIA)
e-mail: prabhatbooks@gmail.com

ISBN 978-93-5521-360-0
MOBILE JOURNALISM
by Dr Rahul Dass

Edition
First, 2022

Price
₹ 195 (Rupees One Hundred Ninety Five Only)

Printed at
Japan Art, Delhi

Dedication

This book is dedicated to my late parents –
Lt Col (Retired) Monojit Dass and Purvi Dass, whose blessings keep me going.

My wife, Prantika, and my son, Utkarsh,
had to put up with my idiosyncrasies,
yet they have been my pillar of strength.

Introduction

You may not have realized it, but all this while you have been carrying the future of mass communication right in your pocket.

The smartphone that you handle deftly, yet gingerly lest it fall and the screen cracks, carries tremendous powers that is reshaping communication as we know it.

Weighing about 150 grams, the smartphone has huge potential that is now being recognized and being put to effective use. It has changed the process of prosumption – production and consumption.

This book will arm the reader with skills that will make them rock solid video communicators.

First, it will make the reader capable of independently developing User Generated Content (UGC).

Second, it will be beneficial for students who want to be industry-ready when they want to start hunting for a job in a saturated market.

Thirdly, it will demystify mobile phones and make it simple to comprehend. The information in this book is bite-sized and easily digestible.

Fourthly, it will help all those who are interested in knowing about the mobile phones, which is today just like a 4 a.m. friend.

Lastly, if you are one those who is yet to see the sheer power of the mobile phones, this book will be a wake-up call for you. Just flip through these pages to know what the future of mass media looks like.

We are already aware that the mobile phones are mass media technology disrupters and game changers. But, the extent to which it has developed a refreshingly young communication eco-system is something that is still evolving and this evolution is at an exciting stage now.

The year 2020 will certainly be marked as a definitive year in which the concept of mobile journalism came into its own. That push took place under extraordinarily challenging circumstances thrown up due to the Corona Virus pandemic.

Short videos shot on mobile phones were awash across multiple social media platforms. The videos, some of them undoubtedly grainy, provide dramatic visuals to the millions across the world who were hungry for news.

The mobile phone videos, many shot by amateurs,

provided fodder for not just the news websites, but also to the television channels. The videos shot on mobile phones also found themselves described as news stories in mainstream newspapers.

In a way, mobile journalism practically covered the modern-day mass media triumvirate of print media, television and digital media.

This significant shift is all the more reason to bring to you this book "Mobile First" that will answer your questions regarding mobile phone journalism and put to rest any doubts that you may have about this new age mass communication tool.

Unlike many who prefer the term MoJo to explain this trend, I would rather go with the term "MoCo", a kind of short form for Mobile Communication. The logic is quite simple. The first term is limiting as it refers to just journalism, while the second term is wide and all-encompassing and it provides inclusivity to the content that is mobile generated, but not ideal perhaps for the digital, print and TV media. All the content that you may enjoy watching or reading about on say Twitter, Instagram, and Facebook is a result of MoCo.

Think of this book as an extension of your mobile phone.

Happy reading.

❑

Acknowledgements

I would like to thank my wife, Prantika, for her constant encouragement. Without her support, this book would not have seen the light of day.

Thanks are also in order for my son, Utkarsh, who did not hesitate to speak his mind and gave critical inputs, helping me to keep the writing simple and straightforward.

My late father, Lt Col (Retired) Monojit Dass, would have been happy to see this book. He is always in my thoughts.

My mother, Purvi Dass, had been constantly asking me to get back to writing a book. Well, Ma, here it is.

❑

Contents

Chapter 1

Visual Storytelling through Smartphones

You are faced with the challenge of turning a complex story into a content that is simple and easy to understand. What will you do? The answer lies in the use of visual media. Build a story that is peppered with videos or still photographs and even add a dash of graphics.

Keep the narration straight-forward as it will have a greater impact on the viewers. Producing a slick video that has sharp editing will make your product relevant and engaging.

Using the mobile phone to produce content that can hold the short attention span of the people is an art that can be mastered with repeated practice.

In fact, I believe that there are innumerable ways to put across a story. But, there is only one way to pull it off and that is by keeping it short, crisp and simple.

And voila! Your visual story will be a treat to watch.

So, how does a person, who is not familiar with this craft, go about creating a package that is appealing.

Well, here goes.

Keep these base elements in mind:

- Idea
- Video
- Sound
- Lighting
- Editing

Once you have got a fix on these, then you move on towards visualisation of the content. Visualisation essentially means how you see the content and the way you see it will be exactly the way the world will see it.

Some people think that if you are technically adept, you are well on your way to becoming a star mobile mass communicator.

There can be nothing farther from the truth.

All great visual stories begin with ideation. The idea is the take-off point for the story. If you have a great idea, only then the best mobile phone techniques can be applied to it. And if your idea is not strong enough, then even the best of equipment would not take the story far.

Even before you pick up your phone wanting to become a content czar, you must think about how you are going to treat the story differently from others. This sets apart the ordinary mobile phone users from those who know how to turn it into a stunningly beautiful work of art.

Focus on the idea. Work on it mentally. Better still, write it down. If you are not too happy with it, then you can reword the idea.

I strongly suggest that you write a single sentence that visualises what you are thinking. When you start shooting, keep that sentence in mind. You won't go off track. The problem many people face is that in their excitement they start to shoot whatever they see, little realising that at the time of editing they will find it difficult to string together videos/photographs to create a composite whole.

Now, we can take up the rather interesting and fun element of shooting videos.

Every mobile phone user is a videographer at heart. I have seen many instances where ordinary folks leading humdrum lives turn into active videographers, shooting videos that are quite interesting to watch.

We will discuss in detail about the various shots that one can apply while using the mobile phone in a separate chapter. However, suffice it to say that making videos is the raison d'être why we are using our mobile phones as our work horses.

Over the years, videography on mobile phones has come a long way. In fact, about two decades back, the mobile phones with a camera were considered a fad. Then, from one camera, the mobile phones moved to two cameras – a number that is still popular on most smartphones. One camera is at the front and one at the rear.

Then, as technology galloped, the manufacturers managed to squeeze in more and more phones. Today, there are smartphones with a staggering six cameras!

However, the moot point is that adding more phones would not help you produce better videos. After all, it is the hand that holds the smartphone and the eye that watches it, makes all the difference in producing the videos.

All those who ask me recommendation, I suggest that you start off with a smartphone with two camera – a rear camera and a front camera.

With video, comes another key component: sound.

Most people do not realise that not only video, but also sound that can make or mar your effort.

Special attention needs to be paid to the element of sound. If you are interviewing a subject and if the sound is not clearly audible, all your effort will go waste.

Another common problem which people do not realise is that background noises can be quite jarring. If you are working on a demolition story, then it makes sense to have lot of machine noises in the background. But, if you are talking to someone regarding another story while that person is close to a building that is being pulled down, then sound clarity will be poor.

The ways to improve sound clarity is covered in a separate chapter. Having knowledge of sound will go a long way towards generating content that gains traction.

Sound is also important even if you are not making a video. Say, you are keen to produce a podcast. Then, you will need to have superb sound quality. You will also need to take care of the acoustics.

Let me share with you an interesting nugget: The sound quality in the bathroom is pretty good. It is a lot better than some other parts of your home. Do try it.

A critical element that is mostly overlooked by those using mobile phones is the lighting. It is a common error that has resulted in poor quality videos, even though the subject and the videographer had time and opportunity to set it right.

If you do not have a photometer at your disposal, do not fret. A simple rule of thumb for lighting is to look for as much of natural light as possible. Let me alert you to the fact the camera does not look at the surroundings as does a human eye. So be prepared to see qualitative differences.

I will, however, share with you few tips on getting better lighting in another part of this book. Lighting is particularly important if you are shooting a video at night. You must have noticed that many videos are grainy, despite expensive smart phones being used. Nowadays, there are software tools that will show you where the light is less and where the light is more. You can make adjustments accordingly.

Here is a tip for you: Even though I use smartphones that have Automatic Exposure (AE), I prefer to set it manually. Do try. The results are far better. The reason is simple. AE sets the aperture and shutter speed depending on the external lighting. But, we don't want that. It is just a tool for our convenience. What we want the camera to do is what exactly we perceive the result to be. So, go ahead and take that risk.

Once, all the videography has been completed, then comes the arduous task of editing it so that it can be turned into a slick package.

Editing is a different ball game altogether and many people hesitate to do it, thinking that it is too technical. Initially, one may feel overwhelmed while looking at the editing tools. However, that can be easily managed with practice.

To edit a video, one needs to ensure that there is a continuity in the video. The video must begin well, have a meaty middle and end in a way that does not look abrupt.

I will be discussing editing skills in a later part of this book. However, let me reiterate that editing is one of the skills that stands between your content either becoming a dud or it goes viral.

The editing has to be taut. In this day and age in which videos of just 15 seconds are becoming hugely popular, the edited content has to be such that it can easily keep the audience engrossed.

One common stumbling block is that people try to put too many layers in the video, like too much text or unfortunate choice of music. Avoid cluttering the videos. Keep it straight. While editing the content see to it that what you want to show is coming through without unnecessary/excess matter.

If you are ever in doubt, just follow the old journalism maxim – when in doubt, cut it out.

Now, that you have a broad overview of what visual storytelling entails, we will cover much of the mobile mass communication ground in the subsequent pages.

❑

Chapter 2

Demystifying Videography

Now that you have become largely familiar with what Mobile Communication or MoCo is about, let us take the first baby steps towards getting a hang of videography, which is one of the reasons that got you hooked to the mobile phones.

According to one estimate, a staggering 80 percent of all internet traffic will be due to videos. Even if we don't get into analysing the data, we can make this out from our own mobile usage that videos are a huge draw.

It has been a common experience for most users that they pick up the mobile phone to watch one video and they are immediately drawn to the next one and so on and so forth. Even before you realise it, you have spent a considerable amount of time watching videos.

The ability of the mobile phone to keep you glued to it is due to video content that is available on it. Whether you are living in India or any other part of this world, videos are hugely popular.

We need to keep a few things in mind about videos:

1. Originality
2. Storyboarding
3. Length
4. Types of Shots

ORIGINALITY

The golden rule of videography or shooting videos is originality. Never forget this. Original work will always get acknowledged and you will notice that it will also get traction on social media.

Never ever copy the work of anyone else. It will find you in the wrong side of the law and it is also morally wrong. While doing any work, always keep your moral compass on. It will be a great guide to give you direction whenever you are feeling like taking the easy way out.

I always suggest that you consider shooting a video as a craft that you enjoy doing. Don't think at that point of time about the number of views. Just focus on the job at hand. Some people shoot videos thinking it will get a lot of likes on social media. It is not the correct way to go about it. It is like putting the horse before the cart.

Even the simplest of tasks can be turned into an original work. Just think about it for a while and you will find something that is different from all others.

Let me cite here an example to make it easy for you to understand. There are a large number of cooking shows that you can watch on the net, but the ones that get a steady traffic are those which help cook in the shortest possible time. There you have it. People do not want a long-winding video, they want something that can be turned out quickly.

Ditto with videos. Viewers do not mind long videos provided the theme/story is interesting, otherwise short videos will certainly do. Why do you think TikTok has become such a huge success, even though platforms like YouTube already existed.

Things are swiftly changing towards short, crisp productions and the quicker you learn the ropes, the better it will be for you.

STORYBOARDING

Even before you start shooting a video, let me introduce you to the concept of storyboarding. Consider this as a sort of route map, which will keep you on the straight and narrow path as you shoot the video.

A graphic representation of each shot that shows how your video will look like is called a storyboard. Each of the storyboard square has short briefs that tells you what is going on in that particular scene and what the script says.

Now, that you have learned about storyboarding, let me take it a step further.

Say, you are a newbie who is deeply interested in film/ documentary making and wishes to start right away. You are one of those who wants to jump right into action, without going through the storyboard labour. There is a short cut that you can take.

This step is far from perfect, but it suffices for an amateur and the results are quite satisfactory. Let me repeat that this is not for a professional.

Just jot down the scenes as you visualise it. Then, break it up into paragraphs, with each paragraph having one common theme. Don't go into the specifics. When you are done writing it, you will have a fairly good idea of how the finished product will look like.

There's a catch. This works well when everything is planned out in advance. But, what if you start shooting a video at the spur of the moment. Then, do the entire exercise mentally. Just picturise the opening shot, the mid part and how you want it to end.

It is a kind of storyboarding in the mind. And that come only through practice.

I suggest that you skip this storyboarding part when you are working on a really short video, say less than 60 seconds. It would be better to just go ahead and shoot it. And if you are planning a video product that is longer, then storyboarding is highly advisable.

All said and done, if you are really interested in videography, I would still recommend that you learn storyboarding. It is quite simple, once you get a hang of it.

These days, there are storyboarding apps available on the net. Try those out. You will find it quite engrossing.

LENGTH

How long should the video be? What is the ideal length of a video?

The answer is pretty straightforward. The video should be as long as it does not begin to drag. The video should be interesting. Once you come to a point that makes you feel that the viewer will no longer like to watch it, then the best is to cut it out.

I follow a simple rule: the shorter the better. Don't use up space on your computer/cloud without reason.

In this day and age, when TikTok is doing exceedingly well, we must bear it in mind that its success lies in the short videos that the users generate. Those days of feature length works that ran into hours are now over.

A simple yardstick for the length of the video is what I call the thumb rule of SMH: Seconds, Minutes and Hours.

Anything that ends in the first 59 seconds is likely to grab considerable attention. The internet has plenty of examples of those. Look at the funny videos. They are quite short in length, yet they grab eyeballs.

Next comes the videos that run from anywhere between 1 minute to 59 minutes. These videos can be fun, interesting, humane or any other broad category. A good example is of a dramatic news development. The news clip, which may run anywhere between 1 – 2 minutes, is watched multiple times. Another popular category is of sports events. The highlights of a football match, running up to 15 minutes, are watched by sports enthusiasts.

The third category is anything that is over 1 hour long. Now, this category is increasingly becoming an endangered species. It is like a documentary or even a film. Only if your video has a common theme and you have dealt with a significant subject can you hope to gain traction on the net. Otherwise, it is advisable to break up the video into sub-themes.

A TIP

While users may prefer to generate shorter videos, advertisers are more interested in the longer versions since they get to insert their advertisements.

TYPES OF SHOTS

For a beginner, it may be difficult to decide on the type of shot that you want for the video product. The shots range from a wide shot to extreme close up.

However, to keep things simple, we will broadly deal with three kinds of shots for your mobile phone:

1. Wide shot
2. Mid shot
3. Close up

The wide shot is what you normally see when you look through your smartphone camera. This kind of shot captures the surrounding and it basically gives a context to what the subject is doing.

The mid shot is useful when you wish to see the movements of the character. It is also effective in showing body gestures.

A TIP

Do not zoom the camera lens to get a good mid shot. Instead, just walk closer to the subject. That way it works much better.

The close up shot is to capture the emotion of the subject.

For example, you wish to make a video on agrarian distress. You may go to a farm and shoot the crop. That will be a wide shot. Then, you may want to show the farmer working in the field. That will be a mid shot. When the farmer speaks, he may express his anguish, which can be captured through a close up.

After you stitch together the different kinds of shots, your video product will be ready for uploading.

These shots that I discussed are for beginners. Once you get a hang of these, one can move on to more detailed shots, which include extreme close up, cow boy shot and long shot.

These terms are simple to understand, yet you may be wondering about the cow boy shot. Right? Well, just imagine a cow boy from the Wild, Wild West standing with his hand on his upholstered gun. In this shot, we frame it in such a way that we can see a person half way up to the thighs.

A TIP

If you are not sure what kind of shot is best for a particular situation, I suggest take multiple kinds of shots. One can take a final call on using the appropriate one while editing it.

❑

Chapter 3

Smartphone Camera Movements

You may well be wondering why camera movements have not been clubbed with types of shots. Well, these are two entirely different elements. Just like chalk and cheese. The types of shots largely deals with shooting videos or clicking images without any movement of the smartphone. On the other hand, smartphone movement deals with precisely that – the smartphone has to be moved.

Till now, we have understood that the types of shots basically focus on what all we can do without moving our smartphone. You just need to point at a subject and shoot the video. What we need is a steady hand so that there is no jarring of the visuals. How to get a smooth, flawless shot will come with practice, helped considerably with gimbals along with a solid tripod.

The types of shots is just one part of a two part process. The second part, which is perhaps a little more interesting, is that of shots based on the movements of the smartphone.

The smartphone movements can largely be divided into two broad categories:

1. The smartphone remains stationary, yet it moves as a pivot at a point. For instance, pan and tilt shots.
2. The smartphone is moved. For instance, dolly, truck and pedestal shots.

There is a third variety in which the smartphone can show a blurry image and then a subject is gradually bought into focus. This is used for relatively more advanced shooting.

Let us begin with one of the simplest shots: Pan shot. In a smartphone, panning is quite easy. You just need to move your camera from left to right or from right to left. It helps the audience see the surrounding. Nowadays, we have also 360 degree videos that are immersive in nature.

Tilt shot is also uncomplicated. You keep your smartphone at one point and then just tilt it from bottom to the top or from top to the bottom. It is a great way of showing a tall building or mountains or anything in which you want to show the height. The tilt shot can also be shot on a subject in which you want to dramatically introduce him or her at a certain point in the video. For example, with tense music playing in the background, you can gradually tilt up the smart phone to show an angry man.

Just try out these two shots. It is quite simple and the results add a certain flavour to your video, without getting too technical.

Coming to the shots in which the smartphone has to be moved, we need to keep in mind that these need a bit of flair.

In the Dolly shot, you have to move the smartphone forward or backward. This can be further divided into two types: Dolly In and Dolly Out. In the first, you can start shooting the video away from your subject and then bring it closer to your subject. In the second, you can take your smartphone close to your subject and then move out.

In the traditional system of videography, you needed Dolly tracks to get stability. But, now you don't need all that. As I had explained earlier, there are accessories which will help us to get a smooth shot.

Now, coming to the Truck shot, which is also known as trucking. It is a bit like Dolly. In this kind of shot, you move your smartphone from left to the right or from right to the left. A good example of this would be a person walking on the street. One way is to simply shoot the subject so that the person moves away from the camera. The second way is trucking, in which you would move your smartphone along with the subject. This lends a certain intensity to the frames.

One of the lesser used shots is the pedestal shot. This entails moving the camera up and down at the same spot. This can be done using a good quality smartphone tripod.

A good videographer will want to use the smartphone to get great shots. One interesting shot that I had mentioned earlier is rack focus. This involves blurring the image and then slowly bringing into focus. Once you do that, the viewer's attention will completely be on the subject. The rack focus has to be done as part of a continuous shot.

As we are steadily getting a hang of how we can create good video products, let us now explore some terms that are more commonly used in cinematography and makes a lot of sense when shooting videos through the smartphone.

The 180 degree rule is a fine example of what all we must keep in mind while shooting mobile videos. The rule is that the smartphone is kept on one side of a set of characters. This ensures that the viewer is not confused. The smartphone must not be taken to the other side, which is called jumping the line. You must have noticed it in movies that when two subjects are exchanging dialogue, they continue to be on the same left side/right side. It is usually used in a wide shot.

Another shot that one can use as one picks up the

finer nuances of video shooting through smartphones is Over The Shoulder shots. This entails shooting over the subject's shoulder. Say you are in a huge shopping mall and your friend is walking ahead of you. When you use the Over The Shoulder shot, it will help to enhance the narrative. This shot can be beautifully used in a video that may begin with a wide shot of the friend walking past well-lit shops. Followed by an Over The Shoulder shot of the friend and then panning the camera to capture the cavernous mall. It can be stitched together for a short video.

There is another shot called Point of View. Some confusion has been noticed when it comes to using the Over The Shoulder shot and Point of View. While the first is actually a shot that has been taken Over The Shoulder, the second sees what the subject sees.

Taking the example forward of the friend at a mall, when the Point of View is shot, it will record the scene through the eyes of the subject. So, just keep the smartphone at the eye level of your friend and walk past the shops. That is the Point of View. That too can be added to the short video, enhancing its quality.

In this example of the friend out shopping in a mall, you can use hyperlapse to speed things up a bit. One of the simplest ways to do it is when your friend gets on to an escalator. For a brief period, keep it at a normal speed, then hyperlapse it, before bringing it back to normal speed after getting off the elevator.

But, you may wonder why do we need to discuss this technique here. Wouldn't it be better to discuss it in the editing section. Yes and no. Yes, because it can be done at the editing table. And no, because we can shoot this through the hyperlapse mode on our latest smartphones.

My suggestion is to switch on the hyperlapse mode when shooting your smartphone video. If your mobile phone does not have the option of a hyperlapse mode, then simply download a hyperlapse app.

The benefit of using hyperlapse mode over speeding up the video on the editing table is that the latter takes up plenty of space on your smartphone and impacts the battery life.

Also, remember to lock Auto Exposure/Auto Focus before shooting any timelapse video.

There is a tedious way out for hyperlapse in which the battery life is taken care of. This involves clicking a large number of photographs as you take one step forward at a time. Those photographs can be stitched together as a quick film. I would not advise you to try this at this stage of learning.

Just the opposite of hyperlapse is the slow-motion, or slo-mo. This slows down the video and can provide a fun way of treating the video. Say, your friend decides to walk into a showroom and purchases a garment. He/she goes into the trial room to try it out. When the subject steps out and twirls to show the garment's fit, that can be taken on a slo-mo to show how it looks.

Let me share with you a smartphone trick that will help you get a great shot, akin to the Matrix shot. In slow motion, the smartphone is stationary and the subject moves. Also, when the smartphone moves and the subject does not move, giving it the effect of the matrix movie.

Do not hesitate to try out the different camera techniques that have been elaborated upon in this chapter. However, in a short video, avoid too many camera movements as it may look jarring.

A TIP

Always remember that higher frame rate gives better results. The frame rate is how many pictures are being taken per second. Also, I prefer shooting horizontally rather than vertically, especially for videos that are over 15 seconds long. A popular aspect ratio for videos is 16:9. There are others like 1:1 and for Instagram, the recommended aspect ratio is 1.91: 1. But, then it is finally your choice.

❑

Chapter 4

Shooting Videos through Smartphones

By this stage, you have got a sound understanding of the technical details like the types of shots and the camera movements. This will help you to go to the next stage of the videography process and that is the actual shooting of a video that is a visual narrative.

Those who are not yet conversant with the strengths of the smartphone to create amazing videos, they must understand that the key to shooting well is to gain technical knowledge first and then picking up the smartphone to start shooting.

There have been instances of people who have shown me their videos and said that they are not happy with the result. Why are they unhappy with their video product?

It is because it is not matching up to the better videos that are on the internet.

Do remember two aspects while comparing your video with what is on the internet. The first is the difference between an amateur and a professional approach. The second is practice. The more you carefully look at great videos, the more you will learn and be able to refine your technique.

Invariably there is hesitation when picks up the smartphone for the first time to shoot a video. One is not sure of how to go about. People just point and shoot, without bothering to take into account technical factors that may impact the video. It is only after you have finished shooting your clip do you realise the shortcomings. But, that's a good start.

Every time you shoot, you will become better and better.

For a person who is just starting out, I recommend the five shot or quintet pattern for their short videos that fall in the Seconds-Minutes category. I strongly advise against attempting your first video in the Hour category as you still have a lot to learn.

The five shot or quintet pattern:

1. Establishing shot
2. Face and hands
3. Generic shot

4. Over The Shoulder

5. Point of View

You can do most of the initial videos through this five shot pattern. It is simple and easy to remember. After you have learnt it well, one can move to the other shots that were discussed in the previous chapters.

The establishing shot helps put the scenario in context. In videography through the smartphone, it is important to remember that there has to be a context to what is unfolding in front of the audience. The establishing shot does that.

There is also a re-establishing shot in which you come back to again establish the context. This can be done after a string of shots in between that focuses on other aspects of the unfolding storyline.

Normally the establishing shots are used to begin the video. It is a wide shot so that the audience gets a general sense of what is going to happen. The physical setting as well as the subjects are unveiled through this kind of shot.

The face-hand combination is one of the most effective ways to carry a story forward. The face is used to capture the emotions, setting the mood for visual storytelling. Let us take an example here. You are shooting a video on how police personnel work. If you take a close up shot of the rugged face of a policeman who has just got information of violence that has broken out, it will show the viewer the tense moments. Focus on the deep set eyes of the policeman and it will automatically lend weight to the story.

The power of the facial expressions can only be matched with the hand movements. While shooting a video through your smartphone, keep one eye open for noticing hand movements, which will reveal what emotions the subject is going through. A close up of one or both hands will show whether the subject is agitated or perplexed. We all know that wringing of the hand may indicate despair so we can accordingly take that shot. Sometimes, a subject may fiddle with the ring on his/her finger. That is also an interesting shot.

The two-shot is practically an extension of the face shot, as we get to show two people in the same frame.

The F-H combination can be focused up on particularly while taking interviews. The subject while talking intently may start using hand gestures to drive home a point. So, when your smartphone is taking a close up of the face, the hand movements can also be seen. That way the viewer can see the intensity of the point that the subject is making. This is one of the advantages that videos have over only audios. In the audio package, one can only hear the subject, while in the video, one can also see how the particular point is being made through the F-H combination.

Can the F-H combination also be used in ordinary circumstances? Yes. The F-H combination can be put to good use in a video. Let us take an example. You are shooting a video on the rising prices of vegetables in a bazaar. When you ask some of those who have come for shopping, they will grumble about the price rise. While speaking, the shoppers are most likely use their hand gestures to make their point. Capture those and use it in your videos.

Now we come to a type of shot that in cinematography parlance is referred to as neutral shot or the eye level shot. In this, we will keep our smartphone at the eye level of the subject. This kind of footage gives viewer the impression as if they are part of the scene.

So, the F-H combination can be shot through a smartphone kept at a distance from the subject, with the smartphone either being kept at the eye level or placed at a higher level which gives the impression that the subject is weak or placed at a lower level which gives the impression that the subject is strong and dominating.

For a newbie, it can sometimes become difficult to carry forward the visual story as they may run out of usable footage. To get over this initial hiccup, I suggest that you go for the generic shot.

In some of the clips, you can shoot the subject who is not talking. In that case, you can use it later with sound bite. It would then not seem awkward, as opposed to forcing a sound bite on a person who is talking. The mismatch would be quite apparent.

In generic shot, the smartphone is used to shoot a general footage that is largely linked to the storyline. For instance, if you are working on a visual story about a flower show. Besides the usual shots, you can shoot a general view of people walking past lovely flowers. You can also shoot some people who are admiring the flowers. There can also be a wide shot that captures the flower show from some height. That way when you sit down to piece together the visual story, you will have enough footage to fill the gaps.

The Over The Shoulder shot is useful when you want to show what the subject is doing, without being obtrusive. In some ways, it is a simple shot and does not require too much technical finesse. One thing that you need to keep in mind while taking this kind of shot is that if the subject makes an abrupt movement during filming, like suddenly turning towards the camera, then that can either edited out or retained depending on how it looks. Normally, unexpected, sudden movements may end up spoiling the texture of a smoothly evolving story line.

In the quintet pattern, the last element is Point of View. To reiterate a point that has been previously made, the Point of View helps show the audience what the subject is seeing. The POV is an interesting shot as it is a kind of connecter in a sequence of shots. For example, if you are shooting a sequence of a person walking towards a shop, you can shoot the shop from outside to show what the subject is seeing, use an Over The Shoulder shot, followed by a Point of View and then a shot showing the subject's face. It works beautifully.

Let me mention in passing about bird's eye and worm's eye view. The former is to take a shot from a considerable height to show the wide expanse, while the latter is used to show high-rise buildings from the ground up.

The quintet pattern is a simple yet effective way to shoot short videos. Most of the video shooting will be covering this. There are times when you realise that things are falling short and not up to your expectations, then you can try out other combination of shots that have been previously discussed.

To ensure that this pattern works well, shoot on the smartphone variations of these shots. You should keep the same shot like shooting the face, but change the shot type from close up to medium.

Do try out the quintet pattern. It is a lot of fun to work with and the results are more than satisfactory.

A TIP

While filming each of these shots, keep the smartphone rolling for roughly 10 seconds. That way when you are editing it, you will have enough footage length to work with. Also, shoot extensively since while editing something looks better than the rest and it becomes easier to choose a particular video clip.

Chapter 5

Special Shots

You must be raring to go and start filming with all the knowledge that you have learnt in the previous chapters. Well, hang on a second. There is still a lot more to learn to about shooting videos through your smartphone.

Let me now take up something that you may have seen in innumerable videos: a still photograph that has been embedded in a video.

KEN BURNS EFFECT

The Ken Burns effect is essentially panning and zooming in a video from a still image. The panning and zooming effect is slow and steady.

The best Ken Burn effect is in iMovie on iPhone. What you need to do is to choose a video clip of a photograph. In the beginning of the clip, you may decide to show a close up of an object or a subject and in the end, you may zoom out completely. So, once you press play, the clip will begin with a close up and then slowly zoom out.

Voila! There you have the amazing effect of turning a still photo into a video.

THE DUTCH ANGLE

If you are willing to do an interesting shot with your smartphone, you can try the Dutch angle.

The challenge lies not in shooting the Dutch angle, but the difficulty is incorporating it in your video.

Turn your smartphone at an angle in such a way that the horizontal line of the shot is not parallel to the bottom of your camera phone. Then shoot the video. The viewer will now have to tilt one's head to see it straight. That is the Dutch angle.

This type of shot is used to show tension. When will you use it? This kind of shot can be used to show footfall at a shopping mall. But, this will not be a part of a regular video. It may be used in a video in which you are trying to tell the visual story of how a crime took place at a shopping arcade and how the shoppers walked out. A strong musical background score accompanying the Dutch shot will enhance the visual drama.

LEV KULESHOV EFFECT

About 100 years back, Soviet filmmaker Lev Kuleshov is credited with creating an effect that plays on the psychology of the viewer. This effect was taken to another level by the brilliant movie director Alfred Hitchcock.

In simple terms, the effect works as a combination of clips, with one clip remaining constant. For example, with your smartphone you shoot a video clip of an elderly woman looking at someone. Then, you shoot three short clips – one of her son, another of her daughter-in-law and a third one of her granddaughter.

While editing the clips, the first combination shows the clip of the elderly woman followed by the clip of her son. It will give the effect to the viewer that she is looking at him with affection. In the second combination of the same clip of the elderly woman, when it is followed by the video clip of the daughter-in-law, the viewer may feel that she is unhappy. In the third combination of the same clip of the elderly woman, when it is followed by the clip of her granddaughter, the viewer will get a feeling of joy.

The Lev Kuleshov effect can be effectively used when you are shooting a video in which considerable stress is on highlighting the emotions.

Go ahead and try to recreate that effect.

SPECIAL EFFECTS

Youngsters, particularly teenagers, are interested in

trying out the special effects, which they hope will make their videos more interesting.

There are apps that one can use to get the special effect. One of the more popular special effects is of guns being used. Say, you want to show a chase between policemen and a gangster. You need to first shoot the sequence and then embed the special effect in which you will see the guns come out and start firing. The video will end with gangster lying on the street.

It makes sense to use the special effect when you can properly embed it in the story line. There are times when the special effects are forced into the story. I recall that in a video, a man is shown walking through a park, when suddenly there is a major explosion and then man can be seen walking away. It really did not make sense.

Be judicious in the use of special effects. If it works with the storyline, go ahead, but if it does not, then do not try to impose it.

3D EFFECT

While you may need sophisticated equipment to create a 3D video, there are apps which can turn your phone's default wallpaper into a 3D wallpaper.

You just need to download the options and apply it on your phone. It is a no-brainer actually.

WHEN ORDINARY IS SPECIAL

In this chapter, we have focused on different ways to enhance the quality of our video. But, there are times when you need to simply shoot with the knowledge that you have to get a video product that is elegant and appealing.

A great example of this is a Soviet documentary made in 1929, called "Man with a movie camera". It shows ordinary folks going about their day.

There are no characters per se. So, we do realise that sometimes techniques are more than enough to help sail through, even if the subjects are practically unknown.

And that is exactly what is happening in today's world. People are armed with smartphones and they are shooting and uploading videos. Many of these videos go viral, even though the viewer does not have the foggiest idea of who the subjects are.

It goes without saying that if Vertov can shoot such a gripping product over 90 years back, then you too can do it. Just pick up your smartphone and start filming. It may well happen that your experimental work may become a subject of intense research in the years to come.

A TIP

While it is good to be well armed with methods and techniques, the best products are the ones in which the central theme has been properly fleshed out and visualised.

❑

Chapter 6

Understanding Videography

Videography through smartphones can be considerably enhanced if we have a broad understanding of how our mind works.

There are different types of imagery:

- Visual
- Olfactory
- Auditory
- Tactile
- Gustatory
- Kinesthetics
- Organic

One should have understanding of these so that you can learn how to stress upon it while shooting a video. These primarily deal with the five senses, which get heightened while seeing those video clips that we have captured on our smartphone.

It's my opinion that videographers are focused more on the visual imagery and less on the others. For a video giving a better viewer experience, one should use, as far as possible, the other imageries too.

Let us begin with the visual imagery that deals with colours, shapes, patterns and size. Now these are put to good use by videographers. For instance, colours are like a palette of a painter. If the colours are bright and vivid, then it gives a modern look, while the browns and greys lend a more dignified look. Also, quite a bit of experimentation has gone into going back to no colour – the black and white.

Can the olfactory sense, which pertains to our sense of smell, be played up through a video? Yes, that can be done. The two elements of the olfactory sense are bad odour and nice fragrance. Let us take an example of how you can use this while shooting a video through your smartphone. Say, you shoot a man walking past a restaurant that says Chicken Tikka Masala. You take an extreme close up of the man whose nostrils are slightly flared up. That shot will practically make you feel that you are yourself smelling something heavenly that is cooking in the restaurant.

The auditory sense deals with what we hear. It ranges on end from too much noise and goes to the other end: silence. In between, we have various sounds, including music. So, how can we play up the auditory sense in a video. For instance, if you are making a video of a visually challenged man, who is sitting on a chair. You can show a gust of wind toppling a vase kept on a table and then show the man's face as he turns his head towards the sound of the breaking vase.

Tactile sense is primarily what we touch or feel. It includes temperature and texture. This is an interesting sense that can be highlighted through a video shot. Say, you are shooting a video of a young man who is working in a kitchen. In one shot, you show him stirring a round bottomed utensil. The next shot – in slo-mo — shows him distractedly picking up the utensil with his bare hands. The next clip in normal speed shows his reflexes kicking in and he quickly leaves the hot pot. The viewer will empathise with the man at the point his hand touches the hot utensil.

Don't be taken in by the heavy sounding word called gustatory sense. It is nothing but the sense of taste. Salty, bitter, sour, sweet are some of the tastes that come under this category. The sour taste can be highlighted through a video in which we can shoot a teenager being offered a lemon. Keep the video on when the lemon is squeezed into the mouth. As soon as the citrus juices hit the insides of the mouth, the video will capture the grimace of the face and the shaking of the head. In fact, when you will watch this video, you will practically feel the citrusy taste in your own mouth.

The kinesthetic sense, which shows the position and movement of our joints, can be put to use in our smartphone videography. For example, we show a man who is walking briskly and turns a corner at high speed. Here kinesthetics comes into play. The videographer will take a mid-shot and capture the movement of the hands, followed by a full shot in which the whole body, particularly the feet, can be seen to be turning. Kinesthetics help in focussing the action.

Last but definitely not the least are the organic senses, which deals with experiences like hunger, thirst, sweating and chills. You may have watched innumerable movies or videos where the organic sense has been magnified. A good example is to show a woman selling vegetables in the summer months. You can shoot the beads of sweat that have formed on the brow of her head. With the sun in the backdrop, she lifts a bottle of water and takes a sip to quench of her thirst. When the viewer watches this video, the organic sense, in this case of thirst, will be clearly understood.

This means that videography is not just about learning the techniques and having fantastic equipment, it is also about understanding ourselves and how we can magnify those in our video products.

Now, you are definitely all set to shoot great videos.

A TIP

When you are trying to focus on the sense, even though you are the cameraperson, think of yourself as the subject too. This empathy will get you good result.

❑

Chapter 7

Smartphone Sound

One needs to have mastery in recording sound to pull off videos that are eminently watchable. By using the word 'mastery', I don't mean that you turn into a sound engineer. However, it is important to get the basics right in capturing sound.

You may have across videos in which you have to strain your ear to hear what the subject is saying. In some other videos, you may find it difficult to follow what is happening due to the ambient sound, like heavy traffic coupled with honking of horns.

In both cases, poor quality audio is the culprit as it mars the viewing experience.

Before we move further, I want you to pick up your

mobile phone and take a close look at it. The microphone of your smartphone is located right at the bottom of the instrument – a design that is naturally appropriate for speaking into the phone.

Here lies a practical problem. The microphone is located right at the bottom and pointed away from the direction of both the rear camera and the front camera. This means that when your camera is directed towards a subject, your microphone is pointed away from the subject.

What happens is this. You capture a fabulous visual, yet the sound quality is not up to the mark.

To help better understand the issue, position yourself at a short distance from your smartphone, with the rear end of your phone that has the microphone pointed downwards. Then record a sentence or two. Now, do the same thing again, with the exact same sentence, but this time the rear end of your phone should be pointed towards you.

When you compare both the recordings, you will notice a qualitative difference, with the results being better when the microphone is pointed towards you. This is how it works. The sound waves kind of travel in a heart shape, with the bottom of the heart being the subject's mouth. So, the microphone finds it easier to capture sound that is directed towards it.

The best would have been if the smartphone manufacturers had made the microphones 180 degree flexible, with the user deciding which direction to be used. When you are talking, use the 90 degree position, but while filming with the rear camera, point the microphone in that direction and if filming a selfie, point the microphone towards the front camera.

However, help is at hand to tide over the sound issue with external microphones.

There are essentially three kinds of microphones:

1. Unidirectional
2. Bidirectional
3. Omnidirectional

Of these three, for a smartphone user the unidirectional microphone is the one we are most interested in learning about.

A unidirectional microphone, which in technical language is also referred to as cardioid microphone, is capable of picking up sounds coming from the front and sides, but has poor capacity to pick up sound from the rear. There are better versions of the cardioid microphones that are classified as super cardioid and hyper cardioid microphones. However, our work requirements will be met through the cardioid microphone.

A bidirectional microphone, also called the figure of 8 microphone, is a kind of microphone is designed in such a way that it picks up sound well from the front and the rear, but lacks the capacity to pick up sound from the sides. A smartphone user will not find it suitable, except for some specific kind of work.

An omnidirectional microphone has the capacity to pick up sound from all directions. One may think that it is the best microphone for a smartphone. Not exactly. The strength of the omnidirectional microphone is also its weakness. While it may be useful for recording something like a concert, in other cases the surrounding sound will also get recorded, diminishing the audio quality.

Once we have got a fix on what microphone to use with our smartphone, the next step is to get a hang of how to use it.

There are quite a number of options available today in the market for microphones. You will have to get yourself a variety of microphones for specific purposes, more so since the microphone in the smartphone is not sufficient to carry out the various tasks.

A type of microphone that you may have noticed is the lavalier microphone, which draws its name from a kind of jewellery that is worn around the neck. This lapel mic is small and can be easily attached to the collar or neck of the subject. The mic is effective in catching the sound bites.

In case, the video clip is not pre-arranged, then you may simply hold this lapel microphone close to the subject and the job will be done.

But, what do you do if you have to talk to two subjects

at the same time? In that case, you will have to daisy chain microphones. This works with digital microphones that allow the signals from both microphones to pass through uninterrupted.

After the lapel mic, another microphone that you should have is the stick mic. This type of unidirectional microphone is good for our smartphone recording purposes. You just need to get close to the subject and point it towards him or her. The microphone will do the rest of the job.

In fact, the stick microphone has two-pronged advantage. The first, of course, is that it will record the audio. The second is that it can be used for branding. If you are working for a broadcaster, you can put the brand next to the microphone and if you are an independent journalist, you can do the same with the name of the website that you are running. If you are interested in terms, this is called the news flag.

Then there is the pencil microphone, which gets its name from the long, thin and cylindrical shape. In the beginning of your effort to shoot videos through smartphones, you will really not be needing the pencil microphone. You can think of adding it to your smartphone accessories a little later.

A shotgun microphone is a good option too. It needs to be pointed directly at the sound source. A major benefit of a shotgun microphone is that it is better at rejecting natural noise, compared to other microphone types.

Incidentally, the digital microphones can be forward facing, which in this case would be facing towards the rear camera. Or it can be a performer facing in the front, making it fit for the selfies.

One of the questions that is frequently asked is how to capture the best sound. There is no rocket science behind this. You need to be as close to the microphone as possible to get the best result.

A news flag on top of the stick microphone can be used for branding, like logo.

By this stage, you may have also come across the term audio bleed and wondering what exactly that is. An audio bleed is when an output of one device becomes the input for another device, hampering the audio.

When you are focusing on getting the initial stuff with regard to sound right, you do not have to think too much about this. Once you turn a professional, there are ways to deal with this, including good quality ear muffs. Ear buds too are a low cost option.

Once you know how to deal with sound recording, you can go to the field to see how things pan out.

One of the first challenges that you will face is about ambient sound or natural sound. Say, you are interviewing someone in a conference hall. You will realise that there is a continuous sound in the background. That is the ambient sound, which is largely unavoidable. After all, you can't record every interview in a well-insulated studio.

Let me share a small nugget of information with you. Once you have finished recording an interview, do stay at the same spot and record a minute of natural sound. This will be quite handy when editing as the extra sound clip can be used as a sound bed for the final audio track.

When you are covering an outdoor event, you will notice sounds that are quite noticeable like a car starting up or the whistle of a football coach. These sounds are quite self-explanatory and can be best put to use either in the beginning or the end of the video story. Another way is to use it for transitioning in a visual narrative. These sound effects can only be got by going into the field.

The sound recording facility inbuilt in the smartphone can only do so much. It would be a good idea to go for a sound app, which will offer a few additional things than can help you get a clear audio.

Along the way you are bound to face challenges in recording sound and here are a few homegrown remedies to deal with those.

If you are recording sound at home, you can convert your almirah where you keep your clothes into a good recording zone. You need to part the clothes that are hanging into two roughly equal sides and not remove the clothes that are on the rack. Then you take your smartphone into this emptied out of area. Keep the pop filter a little away from the smartphone and now record.

In case, you are interested in podcasting, the result will be satisfactory through this hack.

People have recorded inside the washroom, where the acoustics are pretty good. Even hanging blankets inside a room helps in getting decent sound quality.

A TIP

If you have to cover a political speech with just your smartphone, position yourself next to a big speaker. The audio quality will be far better than if you had got close to the stage.

Chapter 8

Smartphone Light

One of the key elements in capturing videos through smartphones is the understanding of light. Many videos are practically unwatchable since the person handling the smartphone did not know how light works to enhance the product.

Lighting as a technique has been a part and parcel of cinematography ever since motion picture came into being. But, it has taken on a new meaning with the use of smartphones to record videos.

That shadows are a result of lighting is a given. However, there is a need to classify it separately since it is one crucial element that may make or mar a video. In the ensuing paragraphs, we will demystify the play of light and shadows so that you can shoot great videos.

Before we delve further into lighting, we need to look at the science behind it. The human eye can see when the light is sufficient – too much light will damage the eye while too little light will be too dark.

The light that is sufficient for us to see is what is called the visible spectrum. There is more to this, but we will avoid it since this may turn into a science class.

Interestingly, lighting can also be understood through the colour temperature. You may wonder what is the co-relation between temperature, which is heat, and light. This is how it works. The colour temperature shows the 'appearance' of light in Kelvin on a scale of roughly 1,000 K to 10,000 K. So, if you are using an LED that is around 2,500 K it will show warm white light and at the other end, if you are using LED that is around 7,000 K, it will be cool white light.

Just a little bit more of science here. There is a concept called black-body radiation, which deals with the fact that a black-body looks black at room temperature as the energy that it emits is in the infra-red spectrum and the human eye cannot see it.

This background of light in scientific terms is important as it helps us to unravel light. Once you get a hang of the science behind light, it becomes a lot easier to take the next step, which is the play of colours.

We all know about the three primary colours – red, green and blue. All three combine to give us white light.

The light's tint depends on the colour temperature, which we have just discussed.

Lighting can be broadly classified into four distinct parts:

1. Direction
2. Colour
3. Quantity
4. Quality

Natural lighting is the best form of lighting. However, in several instances you may be faced with having a situation where there is not enough light. In those situations, you will need to depend on artificial lighting.

If you have the time, space and the necessary lights, a common lighting pattern that is followed comprises of a key light, fill light and the back light. The key light is the main light source that lights up the subject. Since it is positioned on one side, it causes shadows to form on the other side. That can be filled up by positioning a light on the other side, which is called fill light. The backlight is placed behind the subject and illuminates the hair.

Why is direction of lighting important? The direction of the light source will decide how the shadow play takes place. Always remember that shadows lend depth to your visual narrative.

Key light creates shadows which makes the subject look three dimensional, making it more cinematic. If the light is too high, it will cause large dark rings below the eyes and hence are called raccoon eyes. Also, the shadow from the nose will fall on the lip. That shadow is shaped like a butterfly and hence called butterfly shadow. It highlights the cheek bones.

If the light is too low, it will highlight areas like underneath the chin, nostril and eye brow.

It is more appropriate at 45 degrees as it highlights the jaw line.

Incidentally, while shooting through your smartphone, you may notice light getting reflected from the subject's eyes. That is called catchlight and it gives the sparkle in the eye look. Depending on the kind of light the subject is looking at, the catchlight can be round or square.

If you move the light to a side, it creates a shadow of the nose that is shaped like a loop on the cheek. The shadows will make the face slimmer and longer.

Incidentally, there is a form of lighting that is named after iconic Dutch painter Rembrandt who used it in his paintings. In the Rembrandt lighting, the shadow from the nose merges with the shadow of the cheek. A triangle of light is created on the upper cheek.

In case you move the smartphone completely to one side, one side of the face is lit up and the other side of the face becomes dark. This is called split lighting as there are two distinct sides – one lit up and the other dark.

Split lighting makes the subject look tougher and more masculine. It gives a very dramatic look.

The back light can be put to good use too. If it is slightly higher, it becomes more of a hair light. More to the side, it becomes a rim light. This kind of lighting effect can be captured through your smartphone during setting sun to give a halo effect.

Depending on what you want to convey through your lighting, you need to use the fill light, which is positioned on one side. The more fill light you use, the less contrast the image will have.

A way out for not using fill light is by using a reflector instead. The reflector will provide ample lighting.

The background lighting can even be done through spill over lighting or you can separately light up the background. This kind of lighting of the background is important to give a context to your visual story.

Once you have got a fix on the direction of the lighting, you need to keep in mind the colour palette.

The hue is the colour itself, while saturation is the intensity of the colour. Brightness deals with how light or dark the colour is.

If you are planning to do something different, you may consider a monochromatic colour scheme. A single colour will lend a certain texture to your video product. The use of the green colour in the movie Matrix is a good example as the colour is the same that is used in computer coding.

You can also consider analogous colours, which are neighbouring colours. You can set your video in two different shades of the red colour to either show anger or love. Red roses will denote passion, while red lighting of the room may denote anger.

The symbolism of colours is significant. It shows a range of emotions. Do try to shoot your videos using different colour lighting to show the different moods.

In the movies, the colours may swing from one side to the other. Like the colour black is associated with Darth Vader, a fictional villain from the Star Wars. On the other hand, Batman too is in black even though he is a saviour.

When it comes to saturation, it works well if you want to show a period from the past, in which you can drain the colours to make it look like a faded photograph. However, that is best done during editing. You can try to do it through the smartphone, but good results are a challenge to achieve.

When you are shooting through your smartphone, the lighting may not be as precise as you want it to be. In my opinion, we should always strive to make it better by using whatever appropriate lights that we have.

In fact, you do not need a lot of light. Sometimes, there is sufficient lighting available and it all depends on us about how we use it. Just be careful on how the shadows fall on the subject when the light that you have is just a single source.

There is a strong possibility that the only light source that you have will be the LED light that you are carrying with you. Since it is a single source of light, you can use it in two ways. If there is ambient lighting, you can ask the subject to stand close to a window for natural light and use your light as a fill light. Alternatively, if it is night time and indoors, you can use your LED light as the key light and position the subject in such a way that a tube light or bulb in the room is utilised as a fill light.

In such a scenario, getting a backlight may not be really feasible. There is, of course, a way around that too. If you position the subject close to a wall, then the light spill over from the key light and the fill lights will illuminate the backdrop. Just go ahead and try it. It will make shooting videos through your smartphone that much more interesting.

Do remember that you should not go overboard in trying to get realistic lighting. The idea is to have a simple set up so that it is good enough to get the job done.

Over a period of time, you will realise that it is better to use ambient or natural lighting and it is a lot more fun too. It may be a challenge to get soft lighting indoors as you will need to control the quality of the light source.

As far as possible, avoid mixed lighting like sun and shade. Your smartphone will find it challenging.

Anyway, when you are outdoors, do look at the clouds and note how they diffuse the sunlight. That kind of soft ambient lighting is a delight to work with.

A TIP

A simple way to 'soften up' the lighting is to push away the light source from the subject.

Chapter 9

Editing Videos on Smartphone

The editing of videos is an art as well as a science. Among the two, the science or the technology part can be mastered quickly, but the art part needs a lot of time and incredible patience.

What is editing? Editing is the skill to stitch together different clips that tell a crisp, complete visual story, without any hiccups.

Putting together a story is not too difficult with the right tools at your disposal. Always remember that a good editor can make a visual story sparkle, while a poor editor can completely destroy a perfectly promising story.

To edit a story, you need:

1. Clear understanding of the story idea

colour filter on the warmer side. If you are wanting to evoke something sad, then opt for cooler colour side. Do not overuse the colour filters. For a newbie, there is a tendency to try this out and that out. Avoid it. Try to keep it natural.

When you are putting together two video clips, you can look at the transition effects. Preferably use the fade transition as it is effective and does not make your video look tacky. Sometimes the premium ones have transition effects which give your videos a smart, modern touch.

While editing, you will find the B-roll that you have shot to be quite handy. The B-roll is the extra footage that you shot through your smartphone. The B-roll can be used for voice over. You can add the voice over when the video is rolling during editing.

Slow motion footage can also be mixed into the video. Check at what frames per second (fps) your smartphone can shoot videos. To get the slo-mo, you just need to shoot at higher fps and then slow it down while editing it. Say, you can shoot at 60 fps or even 120 fps, then just slow it down while editing. Alternatively, the iPhone and other high end smartphones already have slo-mo shooting capability. So, you just need to point and shoot to get the desired result.

One common hurdle that beginners face is the choice of background music. My recommendation is that you should avoid the background music. But, if you are keen that you must choose music which doesn't have copy right issues. Also, some times the music is so loud, that you can barely make you what the people are speaking. A good way out of this logjam is to lower the music volume when someone is speaking so that audio clarity is maintained.

Once you have practiced enough, you can move on to other skills like video layering. For now, getting a hang of this editing tool will go a long way towards creating a sharp video.

A TIP

The first few attempts may be frustrating as you may not get the desired result. Do not give up. It is just about learning the editing skill and once you have learnt it, the road ahead is quite smooth.

❑

Chapter 10

Smartphone Studio

A logical step after you have learnt how to skillfully use your smartphone to is pursue either journalism or as a communication medium is to start thinking of creating your own studio where you can work at your own pace.

Such a small, compact studio is equally important to help you stay abreast with the latest technologies that you may find useful during MoJo.

Some people may find it hard to believe, but it is a fact that creating a basic studio is not too expensive. You just need to figure out what exactly that you want and then procure the necessary equipment.

For the accessories, I recommend that to begin with, you should not go for too cheap a product or something that is too expensive. Purchase stuff that is in the mid-range and not too heavy on your pocket.

Another recommendation is not to buy everything in one go, even though you may be having the financial wherewithal. Just buy piece of equipment at a time and slowly build up your studio. That way it is a lot more interesting as you get to practice on the new equipment to your heart's content, before moving on to something new.

First things first. You need a decent smartphone with a good camera and lots of memory. That's not enough. You should also have a secondary smartphone, which need not be too expensive. The idea is that the second phone will be a kind-of standby phone, in case a sudden need arises.

The preferred smartphone for MoJo is the iPhone as it has a stable eco-system and the iMovie is easy to work with. However, a mid-segment Android phone will also do. It is just that you will need to figure what works best with it and how you can have professional quality videos.

Once you have got a fix on your smartphone, you will be needing a good quality tripod. Tripods come in various sizes that begin with small ones to those that have long legs. You need the tripod to provide stability to your video. The small tripod is handy and will easily fit into a bag. But, the bigger tripods are heavy and cumbersome to carry. It is advisable to have both the tripod variants.

A third option is to go for a monopod, which is space saver and can be easily used in tight conditions.

To hold the smartphone in place on the tripod, you will be needing a cold shoe mount, which is slightly different from the hot shoe mount that you have seen in the DSLR cameras where the flashlights are affixed. A hot shoe mount is something that can be attached to the set up with electrical connectivity, while a cold shoe mount is something in which there is no electrical connectivity.

The rig will have to be completed by what all accessories you have. It is not as if one size fits all. Depending on where you want to put the microphone and the light, the cold mount on the rig can be accordingly placed to hold the smartphone accessories.

No home studio can be complete without proper cable connectors and adaptors. Every time you purchase an accessory, you will realise that you need a proper connector. If it does not fit, then you will need an adaptor. While some people prefer to keep the connectors and adaptors attached to the devices, my recommendation is that you plug it out or unscrew it and keep all of it in one place. Make it a habit or you will end up always looking for the connectors and the adaptors.

You will be surprised to know that the gimbal, a device that will ensure that there is no shaking in your smartphone video, is something that was written about over two centuries BC by Greek inventor Philo of Byzantium. In that there was an eight-sided ink pot and any which way it is turned, the pen can be dipped and inked. The same principle applies for the modern-day gimbal, which you should procure to get a steady video. Alternatively, there are apps which have inbuilt image stabilization.

Next are microphones, of which you will need variants depending on the kind of project that you are undertaking. Right from cardioid microphone to the lavalier microphone to even the bidirectional microphone, you should consider having multiple microphones since you really don't know which one will come handy. Also, do not forget to get the wind muffs which will help deaden the wind noise outside.

Your studio would not be complete without the lights. While ambient lighting is always the preferred way of using the light, you also need to have your own lights. These days there are good quality LED lights. My suggestion is that you go for three of them – one for the key light, the second for the fill light and the third for the back light. Also, do not forget to place some heavy weights like sand bags on the light base as it tends to be top heavy and you do not want it to topple over.

A light meter can also be used to see the kind of exposure. But, this is not necessary for beginners as the smartphone can be adjusted to get the desired result. A light meter is a kind of optional accessory.

A power bank is a handy device since all that shooting with the smartphone will drain the battery. Keep a power bank fully charged at all times so that it can be promptly put to use. Some people keep two power banks. It is actually not a bad idea since you never know how much filming you may end up doing when the going is good.

A key component of your smartphone rig is going to be the green screen, which can form the backdrop for your studio shoot. The green screen needs to be propped behind the subject. This backdrop can be utilised for a production process called Chroma Key. The colour green is the preferred choice as it does not match our skin tone.

One needs to ensure that the green screen, which is actually a green-coloured cloth, is completely flat and there are no undulations on it.

And how does one use the green screen? Just stand about two feet away from the screen and shoot the video. See to it that the subject's shadow does not fall on the green screen. Ensure that while talking no part of the body goes out of the screen. After the video has been shot, during production, the backdrop can be changed. During production, other technical wizardly including the subject slowly fading away can be done. For those who are into more advanced production, if the subject is wearing a green-coloured outfit, then you need to replace the green screen with a blue screen.

Last, but not the least, you need to have a good quality and sturdy bag in which you can put all the gear. It will be a great idea to have pouches in which you can put the smaller stuff, while the unwieldy tripod can be strapped outside the bag.

In fact, there are two ways to go about bagging it. The first is to have a big bag in which everything can come. This will be useful for long and pre-planned shoot. Separately have a smaller bag in which you can put the bare minimum items like the microphone, small tripod, power bank and other handy stuff. This second bag is kind of a grab-and-go bag. It is always ready to move at a short notice. This is especially handy for sudden news developments in which you need to rush.

So, once the gear is ready with you, setting up your own studio is just a short hop away. It is not too expensive and the quality of the videos are quite professional. After you have got a studio of your own, what more can a MoJo practitioner want.

Happy filming in your own studio.

❑

Chapter 11

Smartphone Production and Social Media

Smartphone communication, which includes smartphone journalism, is finally catching up with the phenomenal growth of the social media.

Interestingly, you may be thinking that once you have shot the video, it would be time to upload it on social media and the work is done. Wrong.

Even before you start shooting your video, you need to take a call on where you want to upload it. For instance, if you want to turn into a YouTube star you would need to shoot your video horizontally and not vertically. But, if you want to hit it big on Instagram, you would need to do just the opposite – shoot your video vertically and not horizontally.

Before we move further, we need to understand the concept of aspect ratio, which refers to the width of the picture on screen in relation to its height.

To put it simply, our smartphones these days have an aspect ratio of 16:9 which means that it is 16 units wide and 9 units high.

Let me stress that the aspect ratio has nothing to do with resolution. For instance, 720 HD and 1080 HD can have the same aspect ratio. It is just that in the same aspect ratio, there can be more pixels which means more resolution, which in turn translates into a much better quality picture.

So, if you compare it with old style home videos, those had an aspect ratio of 4:3. The aspect ratio of 16:9 is popular because it can deal with videos shot in different aspect ratios. So, that is the reason why you sometimes see a dark band on both sides of the videos or the dark band can be at the top and the bottom, without distorting the images. 16:9 became the standard as it could play every aspect ratio and still look good.

Aspect ratio can be used to convey a message by filmmakers. If it is narrow, it can give the claustrophobic feel and if it wide, it can be massive and overwhelming.

But, for now let us simply focus on what our smartphone can do and where on the social media we plan to upload our video.

Whether you are a journalist or even someone who

is using the smartphone to shoot great videos, sharing it with the world is undoubtedly the key reason why you are shooting it in the first place. In essence, MoCo generates video content for existing users like those on Twitter, Facebook or TikTok. You can do livestreaming on Twitter and Facebook, making it a good platform to push out your videos.

MoCo gives better audience reach. Interestingly, the audience is quite interactive. It will promptly ask you questions or leave comments. It is a very engaging medium.

Interestingly, when it comes to hyperlocal news, it really becomes difficult to separate the MoJo from the MoCo. Local news normally gets underreported. However, all that is changing with more and more people loading videos on social media and the community engaging with it. Some of the hyperlocal news actually goes viral and gets picked up by the more traditional media.

A Visual Jab

Your video can be a sharp jab that can alert the online world about a developing scenario. So, if you are looking for a fast result, it is best to shoot a short video that is less than 10 seconds long and upload it on Twitter.

In fact, TikTok, despite its ownership concerns, has become a huge hit in India, where there are said to be millions of followers. To shoot a TikTok video, keep in mind that it follows the vertical format and the aspect ratio is 9:16, which is the same as the smartphone aspect ratio held vertically. In a way, it is tailored for the task.

You can also shoot a slightly longer video, which is less than 60 seconds, and upload it on Facebook. Do try to shoot it horizontally.

Longer than 60 seconds, the preferred platform should be YouTube. Undoubtedly, the YouTube is quite similar to your HD TV so it is best to follow the horizontal format for shooting your video. The aspect ratio is 16:9, which neatly fits your smartphone aspect ratio.

In a way, the YouTube and TikTok are practically an extension of your smartphone capabilities as far as the aspect ratios are concerned.

Going Live

Once you have decided to go live, say on Facebook, you need to keep a few things in mind. One, safety first. Do not try to get too close to a subject who has turned violent. Second, be aware of your surroundings at all times. In your excitement, do not forget that it is a developing situation and things may take a turn for the worse. Also, if you are covering a protest, try to speak to a number of protesters. Try accessing a spokesperson who can explain the background. Even though you may have shared where you are and what is happening, it is best to repeat it for the benefit of those who joined a little late. Lastly, if possible, do respond to any queries that the people who are watching may have.

Visual Clips

There are two ways to consider this. The first is when you are covering an event and you find a side-story. So, it is not necessary that you forcibly try to insert it into the main narrative. What you can do is to treat it as a stand-alone video and upload it accordingly. You can of course provide a link to the main video in that clip. The second way is when you go for an interview and the subject speaks a lot on a host of issues. Then too you should break up the answers run them separately as clips. This can be done simultaneously with your main visual story.

Inclusive Videos

This is an interesting way of giving an immersive experience to the audience is by shooting with a panoramic feel. Say, you are in the midst of slogan-shouting students at a university. What you can do is to raise your smartphone over their heads and rotate it 360 degrees. It will give a beautiful effect and make the video immersive in nature. But, do remember that safety comes first.

How-to-do-it Videos

This is one of the most popular forms of shooting videos through the smartphone. What you ideally need is a room where you can place a table and explain to the viewers what you intend to do. The format is quite simple. You need to have ample lighting and clear audio. From start to finish, the how-to-do-it videos explains in simple terms the entire process.

Graphics

A great way to explain something is through the use of graphics. You can show charts to drive home your point. In fact, you should preferably use graphics whenever you feel that your explanation is going to be long winding and frankly, boring. A graphic practically lights up the screen for the viewer who will now find it interesting.

You can use apps to build the graphics. The bright, vibrant colours will draw the viewer's attention. It would also be quite helpful when you need to demystify a complex subject or even when you are explaining something that is financial in number. Just stating numbers can be deadening, so opt for graphics.

Micro-documentary

A documentary is like giving a detailed, factual reportage of something or someone. This is a fascinating project for which preparation needs to be carried out beforehand. The documentary that you intend to shoot through your smartphone need not be long. It can even be ranging between 5 to 10 minutes. The idea is to tell the story in the shortest possible time. This kind of micro-documentary can be an idea that you have fleshed out by covering different perspectives.

You may be thinking that once you have shot the video

and met all the technical specifications, it is now time to just upload it. Well, hang on there a second. Things are still not fully done.

Branding

You need to brand your videos. Leave your mark on it so that people recognise you. It is, after all, your hard work that needs to be acknowledged.

Let me share with you the ways in which you can brand yourself.

The first, and the most common, way to brand is by either beginning or ending your video with your name and the website that you are doing the video for. If you are running your own YouTube channel/FB page, then share that detail with the viewers.

The Mic Flags are also a great way to brand yourself or your organisation. The Mic Flag is triangular or square in shape and placed on the handle of the microphone. When you place the microphone before a subject, automatically the branding takes place.

Another way is to insert a logo on a corner of a video. You will need to first work on a logo. Before loading it, take a look at the video first and then decide the position where you want to upload it. The logo should not be placed in such a way that it ends up covering up a key portion of the video.

The reverse of inserting a logo is to remove a

watermark in app like Kinemaster. That is not a major issue since you will be able to remove the watermark once you subscribe to the Kinemaster app.

Even a simple title can do the job. You can add a title before the start of the video, stating who made it. So, your name will come right in the beginning.

Now, you are ready to start filming and uploading.

Happy MoCo.

❑

Chapter 12

Mobile Journalism

Mobile Journalism, which is popularly called MoJo, is principally new age journalism that is barrelling through the media eco-system and giving it a fresh, new contour.

To understand this better, we need to take a step back and critically look at the deep relationship between MoJo and Journalism per se.

We all know that in simple terms journalism refers to gathering and presenting news. The process can be through the print media, which are newspapers and magazines, the electronic media, which are the TV news channels, and the digital media, which are the news websites.

In the current scenario, MoJo is like the square peg in a round hole. It really does not fit into any of these broad categories, so it would be appropriate to create a new category that transcends the traditional categories of print and TV and even the comparatively new category of digital media.

MoJo is the 'new' New Age journalism.

The three key factors for its phenomenal growth are:

1. Easy
2. Fast
3. Low cost

MoJo is a different world altogether, and it draws the best from these three: print, TV and digital media. And adds the fourth dimension to the fourth pillar of democracy, which is journalism.

In a way, MoJo's growth can be traced back to 1925 when Leica 1 camera came into use. It was handy and convenient to use. This was followed by the Walkie-Lookie in 1953, which brought images straight to the TVs at home and to the iPhone in 2007, when MoJo got the wind beneath its wings.

The bedrock of MoJo is the same as that of any other form of journalism. Truth, accuracy, impartiality, fairness, accountability and independence are the basic tenets of journalism that apply to MoJo. It is a medium to tell stories. This where the similarities end.

The differences are crystal clear. MoJo is quite a big deal in a small size. For starters, you, me or anyone else owning a smartphone can pursue MoJo. The firewalls are exceedingly low. You just need to have an understanding of journalism and can start sharing your stories with the world through your mobile phone.

The low cost is a big plus.

MoJo has also made news more accessible to the ordinary people. Earlier, only the literate could read the newspaper to get the daily dose of news. Now, with MoJo anyone can deliver the news and anyone can go through it, practically on real time. This is a huge boon for a country like India where literacy levels continue to be a matter of concern for policy makers.

Once you learn the techniques that have been previously explained in this book, you just need to practice to turn into a Mobile Journalist.

One point that I would like to stress upon is that the tonality of journalism too has changed due to MoJo. Now, a number of videos that have been shot on their smartphones by ordinary people have gone viral on the internet, so much so that that TV channels as well as news websites used those video clips.

This brings us to the all-important question of whether the quality is being maintained. The quality clearly is getting compromised. Many of these videos are grainy and at times it becomes difficult to understand what is happening. Also, due to lack of experience, many videos are shaky.

MoJo helps one to give a professional look and feel to the videos. Someone who is properly trained in MoJo will do a much better job of following the journalism rules like giving the context to the videos. This lack of contextualisation can be bothersome as it can be difficult to understand the motive behind posting the video.

This brings us back to what every student of journalism learns in the beginning of the course: the 5Ws and 1H. What, why, when, where and who along with how sets apart a MoJo practitioner from an ordinary user of the smartphone.

MoJo also has one huge factor in its favour that is propelling its growth and that is the person who is shooting the video can himself or herself edit it and release it on the internet. This gives every person with a smartphone tremendous power. But, the drawback is that in a way, you are the judge, jury and executioner.

The ordinary people who everyday watching these videos are decision makers of what stands the test of time and what does not. If your quality is good, your subscribers will continue to grow. But, if you are putting up dodgy videos of questionable quality, then you won't get traction on the internet.

One must bear in mind that the mobile news gathering device sticking out of your pocket makes you fully mobile and fully autonomous.

Mobile journalism is the convergence of technology and the social media platforms. A smartphone is like a one-stop shopping arcade where you will find everything that you can possibly need.

Here is a list of stuff that you will be needing to start with MoJo.

1. Smartphone
2. Tripod
3. Gimbal or use app with image stabilisation option like FilmicPro
4. Microphones
5. Video light
6. Power bank
7. Rigs like mounts to hold accessories
8. Cable connectors, adaptors
9. Backpack
10. Internet connection
11. Apps like Kinemaster, FilmicPro
12. Training
13. Practice

This new workflow may initially be a challenge. With repeated practice you will get a hang of how this works.

By now you must be familiar with what all your smartphone can do and how you can shoot videos that are of professional quality.

Let me first share with you what you must do before embarking on your MoJo journey.

1. Clean the smartphone lens

2. Put phone on airplane mode

3. Check space availability on the phone as videos chew up space

4. You can record more if you can reduce the resolution of your video. From 1080p HD at 30 frames per second (fps), you can go down to 720p HD at 30 fps.

5. Preferably shoot horizontally. Vertically acceptable for certain online platforms.

6. Avoid automatic focus and automatic exposure. Do AE/AF lock manually.

7. Avoid the zoom feature of the smartphone as it impacts quality. Get close to the subject while keeping safety in mind.

8. Smartphone's light can be used, but it drains the battery.

9. If tripod is not available, then either lean against a wall for stability or bring both your arms tight against your body.

10. Look at the lens and not the screen for getting the correct eye line for recording the piece to camera (PTC).
11. Inbuilt microphone may not get you professional quality audio. Try to get close to the subject to get better sound or go somewhere quieter or ask the subject to speak louder. Best is to use an external microphone.
12. Use wind muffs on microphone to considerably reduce wind noise outside.
13. Remember that the shorter the video, the quicker it will upload.

Let us take a look at four common scenarios in which journalists find themselves in during a routine work day. In two of these scenarios, you won't have time to plan out how to cover it, while in the remaining two you will be able to chalk out a strategy to get the best result.

Scenario 1

You get information that workers are protesting at a factory. By the time you reach the spot, slogan shouting workers have already taken to the street. You do not have time to even set up your tripod. Here you need to start recording as soon as you reach the spot. Take a wide shot of what is happening. Then try to get a little closer so that you get a good mid shot. Take a close up of the grim faces. Try speaking to one of the workers so that you can understand their demands. Then talk to the police personnel, who may tell you to speak to the police chief.

Do that. Get a sound bite. Record many short clips. If the police set up barricades, then stand to one side near the barricade which the workers will try to jump over. You will get dramatic shots. Once it is over, got to a quiet place, edit the video and upload it.

In this scenario, you did not have much time to prepare.

Scenario 2

You come to know that a fire has broken out at a building in the downtown area. Pick up your MoJo bag and rush to the spot. You will be stopped at a point by the police or the fire brigade personnel. That is the line you must respect and that is the line from where you will begin shooting immediately. Set up your tripod and take a long shot of the burning building. Also, use a tilt shot. Try talking to the eyewitnesses. Then talk to the fire brigade personnel. However, do not get in their way. Be unobtrusive. Talk to the fire brigade chief. After you have some good shots, edit the video and upload it. Then wait for some time at the spot as survivors may be brought out. Show the human side of the story.

In this scenario too, there is not much time to plan ahead.

Scenario 3

You have to cover a political rally. Reach the venue well in time. Arrange for a press pass beforehand so that you can enter the media enclosure that is normally located quite close to the stage. Once there, sit at a spot where there is a clear view of the stage. Place your tripod and do not forget to carry your cardioid microphone, which is unidirectional and great for this kind of coverage. Do a quick test of the smartphone systems to ensure that the audio quality is good. Once the political leader starts speaking, put on your headphones to be sure that things are going fine. In a separate sheet of paper, write down a few key points and jot down the time when he spoke. This will be helpful while editing since you will immediately know where to look for a particular sound bite. Once the speech is over, cull out the highlights of the speech, do a quick PTC and put together a video.

In this scenario, you had plenty of time to prepare beforehand. But, you had not much control over the light and the sound.

Scenario 4

You have to interview a minister. Do quite a bit of homework. Prepare the questions well. You need to establish a rapport with the subject. Remember a good interview is not an argument. It is rather a way to encourage the subject to speak freely and without any hesitation, without imposing yourself on him or her. Reach the venue on time and take a close look at the room where the interview will take place. Set up your smartphone systems. See to it that the smartphone arrangement is text-book perfect. Check for sound. Ensure proper lighting. Do a bit of light chit-chat with the subject, before rolling. Ask your primary questions and then as the interview flows, ask the secondary questions. If there are any controversial questions, save them for the end so that even if the minister is unhappy or stops the interview, you would by then have a substantial recording. While editing the interview, try to make not one large interview, but rather have a few smaller 'newsy' clips stitched together. This will likely get better online traction.

In this scenario, you not only had time to prepare well, you also had control over factors like lighting and sound. In this you have the best chance of having a professional quality video.

When we do a post-mortem analysis of these four scenarios, we realise that there are a few underlying points that need to be stressed upon.

The news story that you shoot through your smartphone must be complete in all aspects and you need to tell the story in as such a short period of time as possible. It has to be crisp.

Every news story must stand on its own legs. The visual narrative has to be in a way that there are practically no questions left unanswered in the video. Only with repeated practice will you learn the language of visual storytelling.

So, start shooting news stories and leave your MoJo mark on the world.

❑

Chapter 13

Future of Smartphone Communication

Peeping into the future is a bit like crystal ball gazing. But, one thing is for sure that the rapid advancements in technology are leading to dramatic shifts in the way we produce and consume content, including news.

In the future, mobile communication is definitely going to have a different contour than that it has today.

The two elements that are expected to drive the change in mobile communication are:

1. Artificial Intelligence

2. Smartphone processing power

Over the next 20 years, beginning 2020, it is expected that Artificial Intelligence is going to have an overarching influence over the communication landscape, which includes the media world.

So, how does AI impact communication? AI is slowly, yet steadily, making deep inroads into how we create content and also the way we consume it. In fact, we have just got started as far as Artificial Intelligence is concerned.

In the years to come, we are going to witness a tussle between AI and humans and the sparring is bound to take place on the smartphone platform.

In fact, the interaction between humans and AI can be placed into a matrix.

1. 100% human
2. More human – Less AI
3. More – Less human
4. 100% AI

You may be wondering why 50% humans – 50% AI has not been placed in this matrix. The logic behind it is that it is nearly impossible to strike a perfect balance between the two. Particularly in the field of communication, it tends to swing to either one or the other side.

The first element of 100% human is quickly becoming a thing of the past. The technology is changing fast and AI is making us more and more dependent on it.

The second element of more human – less % AI is

where we stand today. We are still having control, but AI is creeping into the communication space.

The third element of more AI – less human is where we are headed for. We will see a quick transition to this phase over the next five years.

The final element of 100% AI may take a lot of time to come. It is expected that AI will be wielding more influence from the year 2025 and by the year 2030 to 2040 and even beyond, it will be a period that will be dominated by AI.

Another way of looking at this is by using a simple scale of 0 to 100, with a moving counter on top. I call this the human-AI involvement scale.

So, if there is a particular content that has been generated, you can move the counter on the human-AI scale and it will show what percentage of it is human generated and what percentage is AI generated.

Alternatively, if we plot this on a graph, with humans on the X axis and AI on the Y axis, we will see a steep rise in AI's involvement.

The larger question is the nitty-gritty about how AI will change the communication landscape. For starters, the creation process may become more AI-oriented. AI is already capable of writing like Shakespeare. In a negative way, we are already looking at 'Deep Fakes', which use AI.

It is expected that content creators will use AI to carry out research and give inputs. In the entertainment industry, we may see writers of tele-serials feeding in the basic plot and AI completing the rest of the task.

For newspapers, AI can be a boon. A lot of thought goes into making the pages. Just think if the news editor has only to list out the stories and the AI helps decide where and how much of the stories should be placed on which page. The big benefit is that AI will take a quick call on the page design and even if a story gets dropped, it will already have a replacement ready. This may well happen in the next few years and save quite a bit of time for the desk editors.

Taking this a step further, let AI play the role of the news editor. Let it take a call on which stories to be given priority, based on how the stories are playing out the through the day. This too may happen in the not-too-distant future. This will be a boon for multiple edition newspapers, where coordination can be an issue. Just let AI help in generating alerts and stitching together news.

Even beyond text, for visuals too AI is expected to do wonders. There is already a marked involvement of AI in content curation. TikTok is an example of how content is curated through AI and it keeps the user engaged. Facebook too leans on AI.

Now let's take a look at where mobile communication, including mobile journalism, is headed for.

MoCo depends to a large extent on your smartphones processing power. Advancement in technology is bound to have an impact on how well you can shoot your video and how quickly you edit it. The turn-around time from shooting a video to uploading it will be considerably shortened.

So, what happens if we steadily keep on improving the processing power? We can tremendously improve the processing power, yet it will all depend on the person handling the smartphone. This really matters up to a point, which may be reached within the next 10 years, and then the benefit of having a superb mobile phone is expected to plateau out.

One aspect that I do not see changing a lot is the size of the mobile phone screen. It may become slightly bigger or slightly smaller. The phone size may fluctuate, but the aspect ratio will continue to be 16:9. The reason why the size may not see much change is that there is a convenience to the current size. If you make it too small, you will find it difficult to see, and if you make it too big, then you will find it too bulky to easily carry around.

All that may well happen is that the smartphones may become slimmer and slimmer and may reach a stage that we can roll it up and put it in a tiny case. And when we want to use it, we may simply roll it out.

The next two decades are going to see a dramatic improvement in the mobile phone accessories. The microphones will become much better, which will result in superb audio quality. The lens too will improve, leading to high quality videos. There will be better LED lights, resolving the issue of poor lighting.

The phone batteries will become better and better, which will be a boon for Mobile Communication as the need for carrying for a separate bank will be resolved.

Even the current broadband connectivity will see a marked improvement, making it a lot easier to upload the videos.

The catch in all this rapid development is that the human interface would continue to be a key factor. After all, the person handling the smartphone will be a human being. Even the smartest phone on the planet will need a human handler.

The larger question is what will happen to MoCo when AI and smartphones intersect. Three critical changes will take place.

1. News
2. Non-news
3. Monetisation

The delivery platform for news will shift from newspapers, TV and digital media on desktops to mobile phones. The way news is generated will also see a shift, with more journalists using smartphones to produce news.

In the case of non-news content, the smartphones will see a dramatic growth, especially in the entertainment sector. Over The Top (OTT) service will see more people consuming content through their smartphones.

Monetisation of the media landscape may see a shift when AI and smartphones come together. Hyper local news is expected to get more importance.

One important development is that paywalls for local news setups will start generating revenue. These local news setups will have a low paywall, making it easy on the pocket.

An interesting possibility is of big news outlets have a flexible system of paying for news. It is possible that instead of having a system of one-size fits all payment for the entire edition, they may look at having micro-payment for specific news the user is interested in reading.

In the years to come, news as well as content generation will democratize and small players will have much more say. The media landscape will see the big media houses jostling for the same space with the tiny, yet nimble, one-person news generators.

The intersection of AI and smartphones will throw up a rich variety of possibilities that is bound to transform how we produce and consume news. The processes will become smoother and a lot of easier to handle.

About one element there is no doubt: humans will continue to play a critical role despite all the technological changes.

It is possible that smartphones that we know today may not have the same shape and size. It is also possible that the delivery systems may change. Yet, the basic tenets of journalism will continue to be the same.

❑

So, it is best to work on your voice and create video products that everyone enjoys watching.

Hum and haw

Let us begin with humming and hawing, which kills the joy of watching any video. It is one of the principal reasons why some of us are not able to do well, if we tend to hum and haw.

What exactly is humming and hawing that can turn into a major irritant in a video? It is the 'sound' that people make when they are not sure of what they want to speak next. It could be a nasal sound or even the humming sound.

This shows that the person is not well prepared and thinking of appropriate things to say. While it may still be possible to edit out the humming and hawing from whom the sound byte is being taken, the problem is compounded when the person asking the question – in this case you – tends to make these sounds.

To hum and haw also indicates a lack of confidence and it shows the video producer in poor light. That it is quite irritating, is a given.

What should one do to ensure that there is no hum or haw?

This can be achieved if you prepare well whatever you want to ask the other person. Before rolling the video, think of what you want to say, structure it properly and then, start speaking.

In case, you are being asked the questions, then think calmly and focus on the opening sentence. Once you get the opening sentence right, the rest of it tends to follow.

One can also practice speaking without making the guttural noise. Take it one step at a time.

Just switch on your mobile phones video camera and speak into it. Speak on any subject of your choice. Over a period of time, you will realize that the hum and haw has reduced considerably.

Pauses

One needs to effectively work on pauses, which tend to lend quite a lot of meaning. Pauses are known to give depth to statements and good speakers tend to use pauses for more effect.

But, why do we need to work on pauses?

A dramatic pause can considerably heighten the meaning of a sentence. The pause can be used when you are the presenter and it can also be similarly used when you are the speaker who needs to be respond to a question.

A great way to practice on pauses is to think of a subject on which you wish to speak. Then, think of a sentence that you wish to highlight. So, while speaking up, take a brief pause before starting to speak that sentence. You will realize that it sounds much, much better.

One can try this out in front of the mobile phone camera with the video mode on. Take a few lines that you wish to speak.

In the first scenario, speak the sentences without any pause.

In the second scenario, pause just before starting to speak an important sentence.

When you play both the scenarios, you will realize that the second scenario with the pause is far better than the first one.

Clarity

Speaking clearly is one of the prerequisites of being a good anchor as well as a good presenter. It does not matter whether you are in front of the camera or behind the camera, clarity of speech is the key.

The viewer should be able to hear exactly what you are saying. There is no point in mumbling something as the viewers would not be able to understand it.

Your speech is clear when every word that you say can be easily understood without straining the ears. If there are times when it is difficult to comprehend what you are saying, then it is clear that clarity has been compromised.

Clarity of speech is not the only element that you need to work on. Clarity of thought is also equally important.

How you speak is as important as what you speak.

What is the best way to work on clarity?

Interestingly, reading aloud a lot as well as reading a lot helps to improve the clarity. When you read aloud, you get to hear the shortcomings and work on those.

But that is not enough. You must also read a lot as only a well-read person can conduct herself or himself well in front of the camera. To sound knowledgeable, you must have good knowledge on a wide variety of subjects.

This is particularly true when you are interviewing someone. A number of secondary questions can be asked if you have done your homework well.

A good, solid combination of clarity of speech and clarity of thought will set you apart from others who too are pursuing Mobile Journalism just the way you are doing it.

Variation

The reference to voice variation is to highlight the fact that when something is spoken in just one monotone tone, it has a lesser impact than something that is spoken with change in volume, tone and speed.

One can feel bored when a viewer listens to a monotonous voice in which there are practically no variations. However, even minor changes can help to improve the quality of the vocal delivery.

Volume is the simplest to understand and control. You must not shout while making a video, but gently raising your voice can be quite impactful.

The tone deals with your voice throw. How you convey the delivery is largely dependent on how the message is carried forward.

The speed of your question delivery or your response to a question can also have an impact.

Let us take an example of how a combination of two of these works. Say, the voice is loud and fast, it may show that someone is in a tremendous hurry and is in an excited state of mind. However, if the voice is loud but the delivery is slow, this indicates that the voice is stentorian and the message is authoritarian.

For mobile journalism, one must avoid a monotonous delivery. Instead, one must practice the set the pace, volume and tone in such a way that it is most effective.

A good way to develop this is to read out aloud paragraphs from a newspaper. The story must be rich with quotes, for which one can modulate the voice. Once you read the story, you will realize that the delivery of the story can be changed with the changes in your voice.

So, go ahead and choose a story that has lots of quotes. Then switch on the mobile phone video camera and begin reading.

In the first instance, read it aloud but fast.

Then, read it aloud but slow.

The difference will be palpable. An excellent way to change the tone of your voice is to slightly lower your voice in some parts and raise it marginally in other parts. With practice, you will realize that your voice has become better and more suitable for the mobile phone camera.

Stress on key words

Laying stress on key words is quite impactful and will go a long way towards making your vocal delivery riveting.

Why should one stress on key words?

There are two reasons for laying stress on key words. The first is to ensure that the message is driven home. The second is for dramatic effect.

The key words are the powerful words that lend weight to your story. These powerful words make the ears of the viewers perk up. The viewers immediately understand that these are the words that he or she needs to pay attention to.

A twin-pronged approach is needed to deliver the key words as words that land as punches on the receiver, quite like the jabs from boxers.

One easy way to deliver a key word is to raise your voice a notch when you speak the key word and then immediately lower your voice back. This in a way keeps the word hanging in mid-air in the mind of the viewer, even though the sentence has moved on.

Another simple technique is to give a split-second pause before speaking that key word. This would immediately draw the viewers' attention to what is going to be said next.

Stressing on key words during a conversation is a bit like using focusing on words for Search Engine Optimization. The better words you choose during a conversation, the better your mobile video is going to be turn out to be.

So, how does one choose the key words?

A way to do that would be to thoroughly study a subject and then preparing a quick list of words that you feel are going to be impactful.

If you are the person asking the question, I suggest you try to include those key words into your questions. You do not have to squeeze all the key words into one question, rather you should pepper the questions with the key words. That way, the words would be spread out throughout the video as the questions are going to be staggered out.

In case, you are the one is who is responding to questions, then it is slightly more challenging. However, one assumes you have some relevance to the story, so that's why you have been approached. In which case, you should try to contextualize your answer and response to the questions by including those key words in your answers. This will help show that you are in command of the situation.

Enthusiasm

Confidence and enthusiasm go hand-in-hand. In fact, they are two sides of the same coin. One needs to strike a voice balance as far as enthusiasm is concerned. If you are over enthusiastic, it would spoil your effort. But if you are under-enthusiastic, then it may seem that you are not yourself interested in the task at hand.

The same is with confidence. What is worse than under-confidence is just the opposite, over-confidence. If you are not confident in front of the mobile phone camera, it will show poorly on you. Over-confidence is even worse as a questioner, as the person you are grilling may get put-off by your over-bearing attitude.

It is advisable to repeatedly practice so that you can strike a balance and achieve perfection in neither being over-confident and over-enthusiastic nor under-confident and under-enthusiastic.

All in all, voice delivery is a major, yet comparatively lesser understood, component of the entire Mobile Journalism experience.

The better the voice quality and the throw of the voice, the better will be the final visual narrative.

One must strive hard to not just have a thorough knowledge of the mobile phones and its related accessories, but also focus on this voice skill so that you are able to stand out in a huge crowd that throngs the online platforms.

An old but effective tip: Speak every morning in front of a mirror after putting your mobile phone in the video mode. Store the micro-videos from say day 1 to day 100. In a few weeks, your voice quality will significantly improve.

❑

Chapter 15

MoJo History

Seldom has it happened in the history of journalism that so small an object—the mobile phone, has brought about such a tectonic shift.

The change has been quite significant, so much so that it may not be out of place to say that this change is permanent and here to stay.

Mobile Journalism as we see it today is a far better version of what it initially was. Journalists have taken to it with a certain degree of enthusiasm and the learning curve has been quite steep.

So, when did it all start?

There are multiple versions to this bit of MoJo history.

According to one version of media history that is largely considered acceptable, NDTV is the MoJo pioneer and it institutionalised mobile journalism in the newsroom. Another version says that the first attempts with MoJo took place at India Today's Aaj Tak. There are other versions too, like a feature story being done through mobile phone at a relatively new news website. But that was not an approach to integrate the mobile phone into the newsroom operation.

We need to focus at what happened at NDTV as it set the ball rolling for mobile journalism, setting the tone and tenor of MoJo in the country.

The year was 2016. The month was December. The exact date, lost in time.

Aunindyo Chakravarty, who was then in mid-40's and one of the top editors at NDTV, walked into the office of NDTV co-founder Dr Prannoy Roy and told him that he wanted to actively integrate mobile phone into the newsroom operation. Dr Roy gave his go ahead, but noted that integration may not be easy.

Aunindyo vividly recalls that day when MoJo found a foothold in the Indian media industry. "That nod to move forward set the pace for integrating mobile phones into the NDTV newsroom operations," he said.

"I had been actively considering the idea of using mobile phones for active journalism for quite some time," said Aunindyo who worked with NDTV from 1999 to

2017 and thereafter for two more years till 2019 as a consulting editor.

In fact, the idea of using the mobile phone as a journalism tool came to him a good four-five years before the day he met Dr Roy and put the MoJo process into motion at NDTV.

While December 2016 can be considered as the inflection point as far as MoJo is considered, but little do common people and even mass media experts know that a lot went into it before the meeting took place between Aunindyo and Dr Roy.

So, what was Aunindyo, who was then Senior Managing Editor of NDTV India and NDTV Profit, up to in the run up to the days before he met Dr Roy?

Though he had been thinking for a few years about using mobile phones in journalism, he realised that the technology was still not ready to take up this onerous task.

All that, changed with the launch of iPhone6 in India in 2014-15.

Great quality videos could be shot on the iPhone6. An important feature that made it suitable for journalism was its good zoom, which could capture high quality videos without making it grainy.

Aunindyo got an iPhone6.

And then began his experiments on the smartphone, which would go on to be a MoJo game changer.

The more he worked on it, the more he realised that he was handling the future of journalism.

That mobile phone practically became his obsession.

"I even bought apps with my own money so that I could continue experimenting," he said and added, "I also bought a tripod and a microphone."

"I would shoot videos with my iPhone and closely look at the results. I would carry out tests to see how the mobile phone videos would look. It was an interesting and engaging process."

Aunindyo constantly carried out what can well be described as mobile phone video experiments. After a long period of time, he was well-prepared.

The year 2016 was drawing to a close.

One day, Aunindyo spoke to NDTV India reporter Sharad Sharma regarding a story on inflation. "Sharad said that he would go to office, pick up the equipment and then head to the wholesale market to do the story. I told him not to do that. The wholesale market was close to Sharad's home. I told him to take his phone and use his mobile phone to do the story. That story was a complete story that was created on a mobile phone," he said.

Another NDTV journalist Sunil Prabhu took sound-bytes in the parliament of former prime minister

Manmohan Singh and Congress leader Sonia Gandhi even before we started using the phone as the camera, said Aunindyo who now runs his own news video channel "News Made Easy" after leaving NDTV in 2019.

"I believed there is no need for the big, bulky cameras," he said, without mincing words. "When we can take holiday videos on the smartphone, then why not use the mobile phone for journalism," he added, explaining the rationale behind opting for a move that had not then been extensively tested in the Indian media industry.

"The basic idea was to get a good quality mobile phone microphone. Carry some basic lights. You don't really need a team," he said, adding: "This marked the end of the days of carrying a bulky camera."

Aunindyo went on to share this thought process and his learnings with the reporters and encouraged them to shoot videos on the mobile phones and to edit the footage on the phone itself. "Use nothing else. Just the smartphone."

After the initial days, Aunindyo helped launch MoJo@7 – a full-fledged news show shot entirely on mobile phones. "We asked at least six reporters every day to shoot their stories on their mobile phones. This was rotated across all bureaus to ensure that we got enough stories every day for the show. The objective was to demonstrate that we could do entire shows without the need for a camera," he said.

What kind of impact did smartphones have on operations?

"Fourteen camera shifts went down to just two shifts," said Aunindyo.

This change could not have taken place at a more propitious time.

The Uttar Pradesh assembly elections of 2017 were just around the corner. The UP elections were a staggering behemoth that was happening over seven phases from February 11 to March 8 – barely weeks after smartphones were being integrated into the NDTV newsroom.

NDTV extensively covered the 2017 Uttar Pradesh elections by using smartphones. "We covered 120 constituencies thanks to smartphones. My assessment is that if we had gone the traditional way, we could have covered only a quarter of those constituencies."

The smartphones proved their mettle in the rough and tumble of elections, passing it with flying colours.

NDTV largely shifted to mobile journalism or MoJo and by early 2017, an estimated 70 to 80 percent of the journalism work was being carried out through smartphones at NDTV.

The low costs of smartphones accessories helped matters.

One could get a basic MoJo kit for approximately ₹2,500, while a similar kit – without the expensive, bulky camera – would cost over ₹1,00,000.

It was also the first time that a media business innovation took place with NDTV partnering with Samsung for its smartphones.

"Smartphones will eventually replace everything," predicts the man who practically pioneered the transition to MoJo at NDTV.

"The smartphones themselves will become very different and we might have special niche smartphones that specifically cater to the broadcast industry—phones with better cameras and integrated video apps, better zoom, and more advanced integrated audio apps," he added.

A question that begs to be answered is why should NDTV get credit for something that was already happening on YouTube where amateurs were already shooting videos and uploading it.

"What we did was to institutionalise Mobile Journalism and integrate smartphones into the newsroom workflow," said Aunindyo.

YouTube had already been in India for a good 7-8 years when mobile journalism began to come into its own.

Once the shift to MoJo took place, it only needed encouragement for reporters to take to smartphones.

The reporters were told develop the cameraperson's eye and once the reporters began to shoot themselves, they developed a fresh perspective.

Why should we have cameras?

This question popped up during a discussion that Aunindyo had with a colleague, Sunil Saini, who is currently Managing Editor of NDTV India, way back in 2013. "The point is this...if they see something the reporter should shoot," said Aunindyo.

But, why are some media houses still using large, expensive professional cameras?

"Because, they are already invested in it. Once the life span of those cameras end, they will shift to smartphones," assesses Aunindyo.

The path had been challenging for the reporters too.

Parimal Kumar of NDTV recalls that he leapt at the opportunity to use smartphones for news. "It was difficult in the initial days. One needed to get a hang of it."

And there were practical problems.

The biggest challenge was that the smartphones would hang after 15 minutes of shooting videos. The reason was simple. In India, the daytime temperature outside—in the mid-day sun during summers, shoots up to a sizzling 50 degrees Celsius, enough to make the smartphones wrap up.

It did not require one to be tech savvy to realize that the only way out was to carry two smart phones.

Reporters like Parimal became smarter. They would

try to stand in a shaded area and only step out in the direct sun when it was time to shoot the video. Then, again it was back to a shaded area so that the smartphone can cool down.

Interestingly, when the smartphones were first being used to shoot videos, there were some helpful politicians who would themselves hold the microphone so that the reporter could finish the shoot. The politicians too sensed the change and realized now that the reporter and the cameraperson were now rolled into one.

However, should all the accolade be heaped on large media houses for revolutionizing journalism through smartphones.

Probably not.

In a way, amateurs were the ones who set the pace for MoJo and the media industry followed them.

Should then an amateur get credit for introducing MoJo in India?

It is a difficult question to answer. YouTube co-founder Jawed Karim uploaded the first video on YouTube—a 19 second clip called Me at the Zoo. Innumerable people took to YouTube after that. Over time, people started using it for journalism.

Due to the nature of the medium and the broad parameters of what is news, it may not be possible to pointedly say which amateur is the first Indian to shoot videos on smartphone for the purpose of journalism.

There may well be several claimants. Suffice it to say, all the claimants have an equal right to the MoJo pioneer pie, which is actually a big one.

Three factors hugely helped mobile journalism.

The first was better smartphones that hit the market in 2016 and allowed the reporters to shoot high quality videos that could be edited on the phone itself.

The second was the low internet data cost after Reliance Jio's launch in 2016.

The third was the internet accessibility to large swathes of the country, allowing mobile phone users online access and turning them into news consumers in one form or the other. The process of presumption—production and consumption, got a completely new meaning as the new users themselves generated content and also were avid viewers.

All three developments happened close to each other, turning Mobile Journalism into a reality that is here to stay.

In fact, the amateurs shot such interesting and news worthy videos on their smartphones that the media organizations, including the TV channels, mainstream newspapers and well-established websites, had to follow up on those stories.

Many of the amateur 'news' videos went viral, forcing the mainstream media to sit up and take notice.

Mobile Journalism in many ways tore down the barriers that demarcated between those who were 'trained journalists' and those who were not.

MoJo turned it into a level playing field, with the person who got the desired video first, walking away with all the online traction.

Journalists like Aunindyo and Parimal contributed in large measure towards learning by trial and error and turning mobile journalism into a fine craft. The smartphone was no longer a passing tech fancy. The smartphones lent a certain edginess to journalism as the roles of the cameraperson and the reporter became one.

Howsoever chequered the history of Mobile Journalism may have been, it is quite apparent that journalism today is in a state of flux all thanks to a small object, the smartphone.

❑

Chapter 16

MoCo Learning

Some subjects are learnt from only reading books. Some subjects are learnt through practice. However, there are quite a few subjects that need both knowledge from texts as well as constant practice to become a master.

Mobile Communication, including Mobile Journalism, falls in that unique category in which you need to learn the ropes first by reading a book such as this one, and then put into practice whatever theoretical knowledge that you have gained.

Before we move forward in understanding over how to strike a balance between theory and practice for Mobile Journalism, we need to deal with a key question that lies at the heart of this new age development.

What makes a good mobile journalist?

This question has been repeatedly asked and there is no one-size-fits-all answer. The answer to this difficult query needs to be layered and, in some ways, nuanced.

Not too long ago, there was a time right up to the 1980s when it was possible to do exceedingly well as a journalist if you had a way with words. All you needed was a typewriter and if that wasn't there, no problem. Just write it out long hand and a typist would type it out for you. For some, this arrangement continued well into the 1990s and for a select few, even beyond that.

After all, knowledge of typing is hardly a huge technological challenge and one can master it over a period of time. So, many journalists continue to type out their stories and news rooms in the evening used to be filled with the clickety-clack of typewriters as eager reporters quickly wrote out their stories on typewriters.

The 1990s was the period when two significant developments took place, one of which was a change in technology—the desktop computer, and the other was the emergence of an alternate news delivery eco-system – the news television channels.

The technology in the media industry got upgraded with the arrival of desk top computers. There were floppy drives. One had to use one floppy drive to first boot the system and then use another floppy drive to type out the story.

The journalists had to learn working on the computer as it was much easier to write, re-write and edit on a computer. The traditional editing system of using the pen/pencil were over.

The technology was comparatively systematic and easy to use. However, there were several journalists who found the desk top computers tough to use and simply continued to use the typewriter. But the young journalists took to computers like fish to water.

The 1990s also saw the first of the news television channels, a medium that required a fresh set of skills to be learnt. Those who opted for news TV channels had to quickly familiarize themselves with new technologies and new jargons. Words like PTCs, short for Piece-to-camera, became quite common media lexicon.

It was also the time when many photojournalists left newspapers to join TV channels after upskilling themselves by learning the craft of video shooting.

At every stage in the last two decades, particularly from the beginning of the new millennium, there has been a lot to be learnt as technology made significant in-roads into the world of media.

Things took yet another dramatic shift with the advent of news websites which gained considerably in the 2010s. Many of the print journalists who shifted to digital news realized that they had to unlearn quite a few things and learn a number of new elements. For the print journalists, work would actually start in the evenings when reporters would file the stories and the desk editors would edit those copies.

However, that was not to be in the digital world where speed was of essence. Also, words like tags and Search Engine Optimization (SEO) became common parlance.

When, we look closely at the last three decades of media, there has been quite a bit of technological intervention that led to journalists needing to upskill themselves so that they could perform new roles. This took place when print journalists had to leave typewriters for desk top computers. It happened when journalists switched to news TV channels and it was again quickly learning when journalists opted for the online medium.

Having understood this background, one can say that mobile journalism too needs to be learnt systematically.

One part of that learning is through books which provide a broad overview of how mobile journalism takes place and in what ways one can pick up the finer MoJo nuances.

The other, perhaps more important part, is to learn MoJo by going out of the classroom and doing it practically in the real world.

A good mobile journalist needs to be a solid reporter as well as a superb cameraperson.

Being a good reporter entails being well-read, having

a sharp analytical thinking, being knowledgeable, having excellent communication skills and have the ability to properly think through the story.

At the same time, being a cameraperson means having a cameraperson's eye for detail and to be able to envision the story visually so that you can take all the shots that are needed to properly string it tightly.

Since the time James Augustus Hicky published the Bengal Gazette in 1780, it is perhaps for the first time that we have reached that stage when two major roles have got merged into one. This has never happened before.

For over two centuries, the reporters reported and the cameraperson clicked and photographed, with their paths running parallel to each other.

Suddenly, here comes Mobile Journalism that has merged that into one. Mobile Journalism has merged the functions of the reporter and cameraperson into just one person, changing the dynamics of journalism.

It is important to remember that while Mobile Journalism has brought about a sea change and a certain structure is now evolving, it is a completely different scenario for Mobile Communication where the organic growth has been completely haphazard.

Amateurs who are using smartphones to create videos and upload it on different platforms on social media are learning by trial and error. Only some of them are able to master the techniques that sets them apart from the rest. It is quite evident that those who are successful on social media have not only got a grasp of the mobile phone accessories, they have also unlocked a major sore point – communication skill.

The super successful online influencers always come across as erudite with excellent camera play. They have managed to up the game in the social media sphere.

At this stage, it would be appropriate to create categories of those who have learnt smartphone communication.

- **Novice:** They have just started off and have rudimentary knowledge of the mobile communication skills.
- **Intermediate:** They have put in a few months of practice, yet they are still prone to committing mistakes.
- **Advanced:** They have put in over a year and can independently handle any project.
- **Master:** They can pull off difficult smartphone-based assignments with aplomb.
- **Elite:** They are just a few who set new benchmarks in smartphone usage. Others aspire to be like them.

The mobile phone eco-system has changed the way mass communication takes place. The learning graph has been quite steep, yet equally interesting.

The challenge in learning MoJo is to keep abreast with the latest smartphone accessories that are practically hitting the market every day.

To stay on top of smartphone communication, one must keep on learning new techniques and learn to handle new equipment so that one can get better and better results.

Learning to handle the smartphone is not easy, but it can be a joy to use the mobile phone once you have mastered it.

❑

Chapter 17

MoJo from a Reporter's Perspective

The shift to Mobile Journalism has been one of the most significant transition points in the history of media, particularly in India.

It makes considerable sense to opt for a smartphone as a tool for newsroom operations at large media houses as it is a huge cost saving measure. However, from the reporter's perspective it is a completely different ballgame.

The transition period starting from 2016-17 has been full of challenges, innovations and marks the indomitable spirit of Indian journalists who brave new hurdles without batting an eyelid.

Parimal Kumar, a special correspondent with NDTV,

describes the initial days of MoJo as "challenging and full of struggle, but also a boon for us now".

Identity crisis

The single biggest challenge—and one of the most interesting as well was donning the role of an ordinary person. The two-person team of the reporter with the camera-person has been a common sight for years now. Suddenly, all that changed. The idea of being a journalist and being spotted from a distance was no longer there as the small smartphone was carried around by reporters, just like ordinary people.

"Stressing upon this identity issue because at the time of shooting we felt at times that we do not carry our own identity and we look like an ordinary person, not a reporter," said Parimal who has been associated with NDTV since December 3, 2007 and one of the first reporters who shifted to Mobile Journalism.

"Sometimes I have been asked by the locals in a threatening voice ... What are you doing? Who are you? Why are you shooting this video? Suddenly my one hand would search for my NDTV I-Card in my pocket while I held on to the mobile phone with my other hand, since I had to prove them that I am a journalist and using the smartphone for journalism," he added.

He reminisced that it took quite some time to make MoJo acceptable. "When people stopped raising the same question that what we are doing with the smartphone, we knew that MoJo has finally arrived."

Time saving

The workflow process in the newsroom has become far more efficient as the switch took place to Mobile Journalism.

Parimal said that at NDTV, "we reporters write our own scripts and follow the basic rule for an ideal script that is writing scripts according to shots".

"So, through MoJo we have now developed a sense of visuals as per our scripts and their subsequent flow. We record/capture shots by keeping the scripts in our mind. These shot sequences are not too lengthy. In contrast, earlier the camera person would shoot up to half an hour for a two-minute story."

Additionally, sending or "transcoding these shots was too tough", he said and added: "Now we are able to save considerable amount of time as we usually shoot for merely 5-7 minutes for a story as we have our script in our mind and smartphone camera button in our hands."

What are the other ways this switch to MoJo has saved time?

"My journalist friends from other channels struggle to uplink shots through OB Vans or Live U app or 3G for Breaking News and I would simply upload it through my mobile network in fraction of seconds without wasting any time," said Parimal.

He goes on to explain that the challenge for "routine stories" is even bigger as other TV news channel reporters have to use uplinking facilities, which is normally not available to them for a run-of-the-mill story.

"So, they have to come Vijay Chowk or Central Delhi where their OB van is parked for uplinking the shots. I don't have to run around as the smartphone is in my hand and the mobile network is available everywhere. So, I save my time."

Inclement weather

Parimal said that during the searingly hot summer season, "The mobile phone cannot bear the heat for long and turns off in merely 7-10 minutes if it is in continuous recording mode."

"I always prefer to record selected shots during outdoor shoots. When I notice that the mobile phone is heating up and may stop functioning in the next few second, I try to move to a reasonably cool place like the shade of a tree, a home, an office and even a vehicle whose air conditioner is switched on, so that a little later the device will have a normal temperature and it may be able to shoot some more visuals for my story," he added.

Video frame and framing of questions

A major challenge thrown up by Mobile Journalism is to do two tasks simultaneously and to do them both well.

The first is to get the right video frame and the second is to frame the questions. Both have to be done at the same time.

Parimal said: "Most of the time I do interviews with the help of a selfie stick. While doing an interview, with one hand I have to ensure that the frame is fine and with the other hand I have to frame the questions as per need of the story. It was a problem during the early days, but now I am confident enough to handle both the things easily."

The next organic question is a comparison between Mobile Journalism and the way journalism was done before the advent of MoJo.

Parimal said that thanks to MoJo a reporter can go live in a matter of seconds, without really worrying about the place. "There is no need for a crew, 3G/ OB van etc. and even team members. I just need a smart phone and an available mobile network."

Another point raised by Parimal is this that even when he is on vacation and he feels there is a story, he can shoot and promptly go on air. "Before the MoJo era, we had to request our local bureau for a camera person."

Piece to Camera or PTC has its own importance in TV News as it carries the journalist's identity. "I have done a lot of PTCs on my off-days too since a breaking news can happen at any time, whether the journalist is on duty or off duty. I can now file stories from my home and record

PTCs as well," said Parimal, and quickly added: "You could not have dreamt of this before MoJo."

Comparing the period before and after MoJo, Parimal said that when MoJo was not introduced, "We were compelled to go to office every day to take our crew (cameraperson and equipment) in the morning, in afternoon or in the evening for transcoding the shots from P2 chip and for doing Voice Over".

"Now we do our job from field and return back to home. There is no compulsion to go to office to complete the task," he said and went on to explain that this, "Gives us the opportunity to spend quality time with family as well".

Journalists are now able to lead a better quality of life, all due to MoJo. A common grouse for journalists has been that they are not able to spend time with their families. Hopefully, that will change as more people opt for MoJo.

"MoJo is not a burden. It's an opportunity. Learn it. Practice it. Use it," said Parimal while signing off.

❑

Chapter 18

MoCo: Growth

The stupendous growth of Mobile Communication in India, as well as other parts of the world, is a clear indicator of the revolution that smartphones have brought about.

As phones get smarter and smarter, with the ability to do a multitude of tasks, those using the phones too are becoming quite tech-savvy.

It is a kind of a tight spiral in which the technology is spurring change and aspirational users want more from their phones, encouraging the mobile phone manufacturers to provide newer technology.

The smartphones and its users have now practically become two sides of the same coin. Whichever way you flip, you will find that the end of the day, mobile communication is a clear winner.

The smartphone grammar

The grammar of language is now passe. The latest grammar to be learnt is that of the smartphone.

The biggest advantage is that more and more users are now increasingly becoming familiar with the grammar of mobile communication.

Whether it is the type of shot, the angle or the sound quality. People now know more about handling smartphones than they did just a few years back.

It is now common to hear people asking the person taking the photograph or a video, to please zoom-in, or to please take a close-up, or to please show this background, or to please pan the shot, or to please take a shot at the eye-level.

This learning is all about the grammar of the smartphone. Most of them have not learnt these terms formally at an institution. Rather, they have picked up this smartphone grammar after listening to other people or watching online videos.

The ability to deftly handle the smartphone is expected from users who have been utilising this device for some time.

The sharpest learning curve has come in Mobile Journalism, with a large number of journalists now trying to learn how to use smartphones and making themselves conversant with the latest technology and the newest accessories.

A smartphone is now no longer just a telephone to make or receive calls. It is in fact an extension of the user who carries it around the whole day and even late into the night. There is no other device that a person will cling to, than a smartphone.

The smartphone has given an identity to many people who have carved out a niche for themselves on the online media. Even people from places with fewer opportunities have got considerable online traction, with their videos that were shot on smartphones.

This trend will strengthen in the years to come, till such a time it does not reach a stage when it is expected that most people, particularly those who are young, have a command over the smartphones and its uses.

Revolution of resolution

A common question that I get asked often is whether we are in the midst of a smartphone revolution?

We are in the midst of a technological revolution that has been spurred by better and better resolution of the smartphone camera.

It boils down to the quality of the smartphone camera. The better the resolution, the better the quality of the video. The multiplicity of cameras only adds to improve the quality of the videos.

The zoom and the high-quality resolution are single-handedly responsible for giving a fillip to Mobile Journalism in the country.

The camera resolution coupled with the ability to store large amounts of data in the mobile phone have considerably helped matters.

Can smartphones endlessly keep on improving?

It is kind of a trick question. A manufacturer can keep improving the battery life. Also, the storage capacity of a smartphone can be improved.

But, what about the number of rear-cameras. Can a manufacturer keep on endlessly adding cameras to the rear side of a smartphone? No. That can't be done. The space in the rear is finite and after a point, it may not be able to accommodate more lenses. The other possibility is that the lenses become smaller and smaller, which may then be accommodated.

The advancement in technology also comes at a price. So, if there is a better smartphone, then one needs to pay more for it.

This is a Catch-22 situation in a country like India. Where something good may force it to go out of the price-range of the ordinary people who may not be able to afford the cost.

Ideally, a good quality smartphone should be available at a low price point. However, that is not feasible in a market-driven economy.

We would continue to see a huge growth in the smartphone market at it continues to align itself with the aspirations of the millions of users who are willing to pay for quality, which in turn will lead to superior quality online content.

Great times lie ahead for mobile communication in India.

❑

Chapter 19

MoCo Classification

Mobile Communication, including Mobile Journalism, is growing rapidly in the country. There are many who are conversant, there are some who are partially knowledgeable and there are quite a few who prefer the ringside view.

The stupendous growth has led to three groupings of users.

The first group:

1. News
2. Non-News

The second group:

1. Tech

2. Non-tech

The third group:

1. Vision

2. Non-vision

When we closely look at these three groupings, we realize that each one of them is kind of an axis which pushes and pulls the development of mobile communication.

News and non-news

The first grouping of news and non-news is also of one of the most interesting. The fact of the matter is this that while it is relatively easy to categorize news and non-news, there is a lot of content that tends to slip between these two.

The content that is neither pure news nor pure non-news throws this open to discussion. It is a bit of a grey area.

But we need to focus our energies on news and non-news categories. It is quite obvious that the content is generated for TV channels by the journalists who now use mobile phones to create content now falls in the news category. Even, the journalists working for news websites and who shoot video stories for their websites fall in the category of pure news. Even those people who run their own websites and upload 'newsy' videos make the cut.

The non-news category is the bigger of the two categories as whatever does not fall in the news category by default falls in the gigantic non-news category. The non-news category is a much bigger portion of the entire Mobile Communication pie. This can be an infinite number of videos that deal with a host of issues under the sun.

Is there a yardstick for the news category?

Any MoJo video that follows the basic tenets of journalism will definitely be a part of the news category.

If ever in doubt, look for the 5Ws and 1H. A news video will more or less have the 5Ws – what, why, when, where and who – and 1H, which is how. It is a confirmatory test for any content that needs to be bracketed within the news category.

The length or the quality of the video does not matter. As long as it meets the rules of journalism, the video will fall in the news category.

The third category of content that can be slightly confusing is pertaining to videos that initially are non-news. But, over a period of time they go viral and this leads to the news websites and TV channels picking up those videos and showing it or doing stories based on those videos. There are several instances of non-videos which has led to journalists to follow-up on them.

The sole condition for the non-news videos to get classified into the news category is when it gets so much traction that it becomes practically impossible to ignore it by the mainstream media.

Tech and non-tech

The technology aspect is a crucial differentiator in mobile communication as well as mobile journalism.

Isn't mobile communication all about technology?

Yes and no. There is no standardized answer to this question. Indeed, mobile communication is driven by technology. But there are gaps in usage.

We all know that all smartphones are not same. The quality of smartphones differs from brand to brand. Even the price is a huge factor. The pricier the smartphone, more features will be packed into it.

Say, you are an ordinary person with an ordinary smartphone who spots something which he or she finds fascinating. The person whips out the smartphone and starts shooting it. Thereafter, the user will upload it onto a social media platform.

Now, consider this. Another person armed with a top-of-the-line smartphone too spots exactly the same thing. He or she takes out a powerful smartphone and shoots it. Thereafter, the user uploads it on a social media platform.

Who do you think would have made a better video? The first person or the second person. Obviously, the second person because the type of smartphone and the features it has matters a lot.

Technology has a major role to play and it is a key aspect that sets apart good videos from great videos.

We know it well that one of the reasons why growth took place in Mobile Journalism was due to the advent of great technology in mobile phones. For instance, the earlier smartphones did not have good quality zoom. This alone was a big factor that held back its use in journalism.

Once, smartphones came armed with zoom that could capture events from a distance without leading to a drop in quality of the video, things took a turn for the better.

The technology was not limited alone to the camera. It expanded in recent years with all the accessories related to smartphones. There was a time when people would hold the mobile phone close to the person who was speaking and point the in-built microphone towards the direction of the speaker's face. That has now changed due to technological development.

There are now excellent quality microphones, which do a superb job of getting capturing good quality sound. Even the lighting issue has now been solved, with proper lights now available.

So much so that one can now build an entire smartphone aligned studio at home—a development which was unimaginable just a few years back.

Technology has brought along better accessories, better software and better smartphones that go a long way towards greatly improving the quality of the videos.

If one compares the quality of videos that were uploaded on social media sites a few years back, to the quality of videos that are now uploaded on social media platforms, one can see the marked improvement.

The improvement in technology has helped to make the smartphones more powerful. One of the biggest advantages has been the longer battery life. Earlier the battery life of smartphones was not up to the mark, users having to repeatedly charge their mobile phone which would run low on power after watching a few videos.

Now, the batteries last a lot longer and even if you use the smartphone for a long duration, there is still charge left to make or take a few calls.

Another big advantage is the speed with which the smartphone battery gets recharged. In the past, people were in the habit of keeping it plugged in at night and using it during the day. Now, a few hours of charging is enough for most smartphones to resume working for several hours. In a few mobile devices, there are super-fast charging technology which takes even lesser charging time to replenish the battery charge.

All this adds up to give a far better experience for the smartphone users who can then go on to shoot more videos, whether news or non-news.

Vision and non-vision

The third grouping is of vision and non-vision, which primarily deals with having a cameraperson's eye.

This is one grouping which is quite different from the other two groupings. Unlike news which you can be largely trained for, and technical which can be purchased and practiced, the grouping based on a cameraperson's eye for detail can be imparted training but not perfected through training alone.

In most cases, either the user has a cameraperson's eye or does not have it. You may have noticed some great videos that contained extraordinary shots. Those shots were first visualized in the minds of the person who then went to shoot the video on the mobile phone.

Vision is a slightly abstract concept, which must be clearly understood. In fact, there are no right or wrong shots. While an ordinary person may see only the ordinariness in something that he or she is seeing, a person with a cameraperson's eye will be quick to notice the extraordinariness.

How to develop the cameraperson's eye?

Training can help to a great extent, but the only way out to develop this unique trait is by looking for that way to shoot the video, which others may not do.

Even if you are an untrained person, it greatly helps if you can shoot a part of the video from a higher angle. This lends a certain depth to the visual narrative.

You can also use other camera shots that have been explained in a different chapter of this book. Those too will give a certain tonality to your video.

A video with great shots which dazzle can only be from a cameraperson's eye. Online platforms are peppered with videos, most of which are plain and not exciting. There are only the few distinct videos where there is a certain uniqueness and something different that you remember it even after a long time especially when the public memory these days is short-term.

There is also a word of caution. Many people think that simply by inserting complex shots into the video one can show that one has a cameraperson's eye. It is not so. Even simple shots too work brilliantly.

While shooting on the mobile phone, a simple decision to switch to a close-up from a mid-section shot can make all the difference.

Essentially, you should strive to look at what is unfolding in front of you in an objective manner and visualize how you want to use your mobile phone. This works pretty well if one has time on hand and can then plan out the shot.

It is best not to think too much about the cameraperson's eye, since there is little one can do if one does not have it. There is no need to feel disappointed if you realize that there is nothing special in video after video that you are shooting. Best is to use your knowledge, your technical skills and your superior equipment to score over others.

Now that we have looked closely at the three groupings—news and non-news, tech and non-tech as well as vision and non-vision, that can be used as differentiators, we need to also take stock of what happens when a user has either two or just one of these three factors.

Let me share eight of the combinations that are relevant for mobile communication. Four have been selected from the non-news category, which will largely take care of mobile communication per se and four from the news category that will take care of Mobile Journalism.

Here are the classifications for non-news:

- **Non-news, non-tech, non-vision:** This type of mobile phone user does not really have a nose for news. This user is not friendly with technology and also lacks the cameraperson's eye. The quality of videos from this user would be very poor.
- **Non-news, non-tech, vision:** This type of mobile phone user is not the one who is looking for newsy stuff and also does not have a high-end mobile phone. However, this person has that critical cameraperson's eye which sets him or her apart from others. The video quality may be poor, but it is bound to be quite watchable.
- **Non-news, tech, non-vision:** This type of mobile phone user too does not have a news sense and also does not have a cameraperson's eye. But he or she has a powerful smartphone and lots of accessories.

The videos from him or her will be technically of good quality. There are high chances of this user producing videos that are far from exciting.

- **Non-news, tech, vision:** This type of mobile phone user has no understanding of what is news. However, he or she has good smartphone and accessories as well as a cameraperson's eye. These videos are going to be of high quality and very watchable so much so that some of them may also go viral. In fact, many of the videos on the internet today fall in this category.

Here are the classifications for the news category:

- **News, non-tech, non-vision:** This type of mobile phone user has a nose for news. However, what he or she is sorely lacking is a powerful smartphone as well as a cameraperson's eye. The video quality may not be up to the mark, but the videos will meet the basic parameters to fall in the news category.
- **News, tech, non-vision:** This type of mobile phone user has a solid understanding of news. He or she is also armed with good quality mobile phone. But, this user does not have the cameraperson's eye. The technical quality of video will be good and the videos will fall in the news category. The shortcoming of the videos will be in that 'X' factor that can come only with a user with a cameraperson's eye.
- **News, non-tech, vision:** This type of mobile phone user knows all about news. This user does have the crucial cameraperson's eye, but what he or she lacks

is a good smartphone along with the accessories. The quality of videos may not be up to the mark, yet the videos are going to be quite watchable. In fact, in the early days of Mobile Journalism, many journalists did not have good smartphones, yet what they shot went on air. It was simply because in the 24/7 news industry, even a grainy video is fair game, as long as it is news.

- **News, tech, vision:** This type of the mobile phone user can be considered by one of the top two best combinations. The other combination at par is non-news, tech and vision. This user has a solid understanding of news. He or she also has a first-class smartphone and accessories. This user in addition has a clear cameraperson's eye. The video quality will be so good that it would be a pleasure to watch it. It is highly recommended that new users watch these videos so that they can learn from it.

Almost all the mobile phone users can be classified on the basis of the matrix that has been shared here.

One needs to see into which category one is falling and those who are really interested, should strive to move on to the best of that category. A shift from one category to another takes time. Say, you are currently operating in the non-news, non-tech and vision category and would like to move to the news, tech and vision category. You would have to work towards not only learning the nuances of news, you would also have to steadily start acquiring a great smartphone along with the accessories.

Any user needs to be patient while making this shift as things take quite a bit of time. Even if you have a high-quality smartphone and the accessories are newly purchased, you will need to give yourself time to familiarize yourself with the mobile phone accessories.

It is advisable that while transitioning from one category to another, the mobile phone user should keep abreast with what is happening in the world of mobile telephony. Also, watch videos of the category that you wish to move to. There may be hidden gems that you spot and learn from those.

If you are student who is pursuing mass media, aim for the best category of having a strong news sense coupled with a great smartphone. Try developing a cameraperson's eye.

If you are a student who only wishes to master mobile communication, then aspire to be the best in the non-news category with a solid smartphone. You too need to try developing a cameraperson's eye.

When you are holding the smartphone in your hand, try to shoot videos that are excellent. You really do not know whether the videos are going to go viral or not. There are innumerable users who did not even realize that the videos shot on their mobile phone had gone viral.

Always strive for the best when you shoot on your smartphone.

❑

Machine theory of mass communication states that as mass communication begins to rely more and more on computer-based Artificial Intelligence, it will gradually lose its organic state and become synthetic in nature.

The four elements of mass communication content – Video, Audio, Images, Text (VAIT) – are deeply influenced by the computer-generated processes.

One way of tracking this is through the Human-AI mass communication content scale, which is essentially a simple scale that is marked 0 to 100, with a moving counter on top.

So, if there is a particular content that has been

generated, the counter on the Human-AI scale will show what percentage of it is human generated and what percentage is AI generated.

As time passes, the scale will gradually begin to tilt in favour of AI-generated content.

If we plot this on a graph, with humans on the X axis and AI on the Y axis, we will note a steep rise in AI's involvement over a period of time.

X (Human generated content) will be inversely proportional to Y (AI generated content).

$$X \propto Y$$

So, as machines start generating more content, the human factor will keep on reducing.

This will hold true for content generation as well content dissemination.

The overt dependence on machines like computers to make life easy for humans will gradually make life more difficult as it will become virtually impossible to differentiate between human generated and machine generated content.

This theory applies equally over Video, Audio, Images and Text.

Machines are already active in content delivery, with AI now choosing what we see on our devices – the mobile phones, laptops and desktops.

Machines are also generating content, like the deeply troubling deep fakes – something that is practically impossible to spot as machine-generated for an untrained eye.

The machine theory of mass communication fleshes out the interplay between humans and their machines.

❑

The year 2020 is going to be a tipping point in the media eco-system, marked by an exponential and explosive growth of Mobile Communication in general and Mobile Journalism in particular.

More and more people are now moving towards their mobile phone to get their daily dose of news and views. The Covid-19 pandemic has hastened a seemingly irreversible process that has seen people ditching the more traditional media and opting for their smartphones.

Mobile Communication as we know it today is also going to transform. The popular apps that are ruling the roost may lose to a newbie. The rapid advancement in technology means that what is relevant now may quickly become irrelevant tomorrow.

The rise of MoCo and MoJo also means that individualism is now par for the course. You are practically on your own in this highly networked world. It is dichotomous in nature since you are all alone when it comes to generating and uploading content, yet you are not exactly alone since you are connected to the online world 24/7.

The communication world is changing. Something new or exciting is keeping us hooked all the time to our smartphone.

The common denominator is that content, whether it is news or non-news, is a much sought after commodity. The challenge is to monetize it.

Smartphones are democratizing content. Shooting videos on a smartphone is cheap, drastically bringing down the production cost. This in turn translates into lower running cost to operate any content driven outfit.

The larger question is whether the viewer will be willing to pay for content, particularly if it has been shot on a smartphone and perhaps does not provide the same level of professional quality that expensive cameras can provide.

One can hazard a calculated guess that there will always be a demand for good quality content. This is true for non-news as well as news categories. The OTT platforms have emerged as a solid alternative that provide content of all hues at costs that are quite affordable.

In fact, the annual subscription fee of a content-rich OTT platform equals the cost incurred by a family going out for one movie. It is not rocket science to understand that content delivered through smartphones are working out to be quite cheap and good. It is value for money.

Without a shred of doubt, one can say that the smartphone is the future of all hues of communication.

Happy smartphone filming.

❑